PADRE KINO

And the Trail to the Pacific

Territory explored by Padre Eusebio Francisco Kino

Padre Kino

And the Trail to the Pacific

By
Jack Steffan

With paintings by José Cirilo Ríos Ramos

Hillside Education

Hillside Education
475 Bidwell Hill Road
Lake Ariel, PA 18436
www.hillsideeducation.com

CONTENTS

Cast of Characters

JESUITS:

Padre Gonzalez

Padre Polici

Padre Picolo

Padre Salvatierra, *missionary who visited Kino in Sonora, went to California, finally became provincial in Mexico City*

Padre Campos, *missionary at San Ignacio*

Padre Saeta, *missionary at Caborca*

Padre Minutuli, *missionary at Tubutama*

Padre Velarde, *assistant to Kino at Dolores*

Padre Eusebio Francisco Kino, *explorer and map maker, founder of missions in California and Sonora*

SPANISH ARMY OFFICERS:

General Jironza, *commandant at San Juan*

Lieutenant Juan Manje, *his nephew and close friend of Padre Kino*

Lieutenant Antonio Solis, *commanding officer of the Flying Column*

Captain Carrasco, *military observer of one of Kino's expeditions*

INDIANS:

Chief Ibo, *California tribe*

Hulo, *his son*

Chief Coxi, *first captain general at Mission Dolores (Pima)*

Francisco, *interpreter (Pima-Spanish)*

Chief Soba, *from the region near Caborca (Pima)*

Chief Felipe, *from region near Magdalena (Pima)*

Marcos, *son of another captain general at Mission Dolores (Pima)*

Chief Coro, *of Quiburi (tribe related to Pimas)*

Chief Duck Tail, *of Cocospora (Pima)*

Chief Humari, *of Ojio, neighbor to Coro (tribe related to Pimas)*

PADRE KINO

And the Trail to the Pacific

Padre Kino and Admiral Atondo in California

Chapter 1

CALIFORNIA MISSION

[1685]

At an altar set up in front of a tiny unfinished adobe chapel, near San Bruno, in Lower California, Padre Eusebio Francisco Kino was finishing the saying of his Mass. His vestments were the red of a stormy sunrise and in them his sturdy figure looked taller, more commanding than usual as he turned to bless the Spanish admiral and his soldiers who knelt on the sun-baked earth.

During the rest of the day the good padre would bustle about in a rumpled black robe not seeming to care how he looked. But for the Mass all must be beautiful—embroidered vestments, white cloth of finest linen, the chime of silver bells at the Consecration, and the chalice held above his head, golden, sparkling with gems.

Did he think such things impressed these dirty California savages? wondered one of the soldiers, edging into a patch of shade beside a thornbush. He felt half undressed without armor or weapons, but Padre Kino had ordered them laid aside when Mass was said. Of course, in this blistering sun it was as well not to wear armor. A man could bake inside it like bread in an oven. The wind that blew from the east across the Sea of California was dry and hot as if the long rolling swells were desert sand instead of water.

The soldier licked his cracked lips and tried to swallow, but his throat was parched. Would he ever taste good water again, he wondered, or have enough of it to drink? This was a cursed country. Spain would be better off without it. For a hundred and fifty years, ever since the days of Cortez, the Spanish had been trying to establish a settlement on this great "Island of California." Now, in 1685, it was still desolate, peopled only by savages and a handful of white men.

He edged closer to the thorn tree and turned a little to eye a sizeable group of Indians. Look at them, pretending to be devout! Some were even kneeling. There was Chief Ibo, who had come only yesterday from a village twenty leagues (about fifty miles) down the coast, and his tall son beside him, both as naked as the day they were born. How could Padre Kino trust such heathens? Calling them his children and going fearlessly among the wildest of them—it made your skin crawl just to think of it.

"Animals," gritted the soldier. "Kino may think they are human beings, with souls like his own, but they are nothing more than dirty, treacherous animals!"

As if his muttered words had triggered it, a scream sliced the stillness. The soldier leaped to his feet, snatching wildly for a weapon that was not there, and jumped back as a black dog streaked past him into the thorn patch. He was almost knocked off his feet by the tall young Indian crashing after it, blood streaming from his slashed leg.

Indians and soldiers milled apart in two noisy, frightened groups. At the altar Padre Kino's vestments swirled in a cloud of red. He shouted, but no one heard. A rock hurtled through the air toward the soldiers and from somewhere came the explosion of an arquebus, the gun then used by the Spaniards. The Indians fled in a cloud of dust. Soldiers stood guiltily silent.

"Who fired that gun?" Padre Kino's face was white with anger. "You were ordered to come here without weapons. Admiral Atondo, find that man and have him punished!"

"I was wishing for a weapon of my own," muttered the admiral, but he was careful to say it under his breath. Padre Kino was a brilliant mathematician, the only maker of maps in the New World and the official cartographer of his expedition. *How could such a learned man be so impractical when it came to dealing with savages?* the admiral wondered.

"Whose dog was that?" the padre demanded now. "The first time these Indians show reverence for God, what happens? One of you does not tie up his worthless mongrel. How often must I tell you that we have to love these people before we can expect them to love God? Kneel, all of you, while I pray that He may not permit all our work to be destroyed by one foolish accident."

As the soldiers went down on their knees, the one by the thornbush heard a whisper of bare foot on sand, saw a brown face peer through the dusty leaves. The soldier stayed where he was when the rest of his companions hurried off to their quarters and watched the young Indian move stealthily into the open as Padre Kino turned to fold the white altar cloth. The soldier looked for a stick, a stone, something to throw. But without looking up Padre Kino said, "Peace, my son. He means no harm."

"How do you know?" the soldier growled.

"His father is my friend," said Kino serenely and went on smoothing the cloth until the boy was not two steps away. Then Padre Kino turned, smiling.

"So, young Hulo, you are hurt. Let me see." He spoke in Spanish, but no one could mistake his meaning. The boy stood motionless as Kino stooped to examine the leg.

"It is not deep, this wound. Come with me and I will wash it."

The boy edged away, but Kino's strong, square fingers gripped the bare arm. "Come," he said again, this time in the boy's own language. "I will give you food."

The black eyes widened. Food, this strange man said. No one from Hulo's village ever had enough to eat. He followed through a low doorway into a small adobe building. Padre Kino rummaged in a sack for a handful of dried maize, noting with a frown how little was left. If a boat did not manage to cross the stormy Sea of California within the next week or so, the garrison would be hungrier than the Indians.

The padre poured brackish water into a bowl and washed the bitten leg while Hulo chewed the parched corn. The bite was nothing. Village dogs were always biting. It was the suddenness of the attack that had startled him. His black eyes watched every move as Kino took off the beautiful red vestments and put them carefully in a wooden chest, set the chalice gently in another chest and locked it.

"Come," said Kino, "now both of us will eat," and led the way outside. Around the corner, in the shade of the rough adobe wall, a half dozen Indian boys of all sizes squatted around a bowl on the sandy earth, pushing pieces of raw fish into their mouths as fast as they could swallow. The smallest of them saw Kino, jumped up and threw both arms around the black-robed knees, jabbering a mixture of Spanish and Indian that Hulo could not make out. Kino seemed to understand.

"After we have eaten," he said, "I will tell you about Our Lord, and you will help this new one learn the Ave Maria."

The padre's food was a mixture of raw herbs and seeds ground fine, and he ate little of that. For two years he had fasted, worked and prayed with the Indians of Lower California. He had explored the mountains, drawn maps of the eastern coast line, and, as pathfinder for Admiral Atondo, had led the party westward across the peninsula to the shores of the great Pacific Ocean. They were the first white men to make such a crossing and Kino recorded it, as he did all his travels, by charting the course and making a map which showed in detail every place they visited. He enjoyed everything connected with such an expedition, even the hardships.

But above all, he was a missionary, and his first care was the Indians. At San Bruno he had built a church and a small house for the Jesuits, planted fruit trees, maize and melons, all with the cheerful help of the Indians. His crops had flourished for a time, but the long drought and a rare frost or two had ruined everything. On his expeditions with the soldiers he had constantly been in search of a more suitable place for a permanent mission.

Padre Kino sighed. Yesterday the admiral had said there was no hope for a permanent settlement unless his divers found many more pearls in the California waters. Kino felt sure that they would never find enough pearls to pay the expenses of settlement and defense. It took great quantities of supplies to feed even a small garrison. At times in the last two years the soldiers had nearly starved when ships could not cross the stormy waters between Lower California and the Mexican mainland. Now the orchard trees had dried to brown sticks; no vegetables grew in the parched gardens; the maize had not even sprouted in the small dusty fields. And once again the supply ship was late in coming.

Padre Kino shrugged away his gloomy thoughts and smiled at Hulo. These Indian youngsters knew he loved them. Why else would they leave their families and come to live with him? He could not go anywhere without a troop of them running alongside.

Hulo soon became the leader of the band of Indian boys. Within a month, when the ship finally made the crossing, he helped the soldiers unload bags of corn and wheat from the small boat that brought them to shore. When Kino saw that barely enough food had come for the soldiers much less for his Indians, he decided to go to the mainland himself in search of extra supplies. So when the ship sailed again the padre was on board and Hulo went with him. Despite the tossing, pitching waters off the coast which cast fear even into the hearts of the seasoned sailors, the Indian lad seemed quite unafraid of any danger so long as he was with his Padre Kino.

For three days the wind blew so hard out of the east, the ship bobbed up and down without making any headway. They could still see the mountains of Lower California on the morning of the fourth day, but then the wind shifted, the sails filled. They began to climb the towering waves, dip into the troughs between. Slowly the ship moved east toward Mexico. By afternoon the sea was calmer and Padre Kino, with Hulo beside him, sat on the deck, working on a map of California.

The captain disliked all Indians. He pretended Hulo was not there as he stopped to watch.

"How do you know where to put the bay?" asked the captain.

"I learned the making of maps as you learned the business of sailing a ship." The square fingers kept on with the painstaking task until "Bahia de La Paz," the Bay of Peace, was lettered in the lower left-hand corner.

Padre Kino straightened with a sigh. "It is too bad we did not keep the peace for which the bay was named."

"How can you keep peace with savages?" snorted the captain. "It will be well when we Spanish give up all idea of a California colony."

"Do not say that." Kino's blue-gray eyes darkened.

"Why not? In Mexico there is great wealth, with much gold and silver. California has nothing but savages."

"But each of them has a soul," reminded the padre. "There is nothing more precious than a human soul. If only I could baptize all these Indians!"

"You had better not," said the captain grimly. "Remember what happened when you baptized the old man at San Bruno, and he died? The Indians said you were a bad doctor. They wanted to kill you, and the rest of us, too."

"But that man went straight to heaven," said Kino serenely. "If we find an Indian in danger of death we always baptize him. It is the strong young ones like Hulo here that we may not baptize until they are more fully instructed. And how can we do this until we establish a permanent mission among his people. How is he to learn about God and the Church?"

The captain grunted. "You think more of a dirty savage than you do of your own skin."

"Why, of course I do." Kino looked up in surprise. "That is the reason I became a Jesuit, so I could come as a missionary to people like these. I would give my life gladly for them. Is not that what Our Lord did for us?"

The captain sniffed, but was silent until Kino began to

sketch a picture of two Indians in the upper left- hand corner of the map, then he said suddenly, "What do you do there? Oh, I see. It is the region north of California which has not been explored. You do not know what is there, so you make a decoration to fill that corner."

"Very good," smiled Kino. "No one knows what is to the north. When I was a student in Germany, my professors taught me that California is a peninsula. Now everyone believes what the English explorer, Sir Francis Drake, said, that California is an island. But I am still not sure—"

He looked up at the white clouds sailing so smoothly across the blue sky. "It would be wonderful to find that my professors were right. Just think—if we could bring provisions overland to the California settlements, we would not have to worry about stormy seas and leaky ships!"

"You would like to see me lose my employment?" cried the captain. "Well, let me tell you, Padre, I would be glad to go elsewhere. And you think we make great profits bringing supplies to California? It is not true. The owners of these ships and every man who sails in them would be happy if they never heard the name California again!" And he stamped off to take the wheel.

For the rest of the voyage the weather was pleasant, the winds westerly and brisk. When they docked at the little Mexican port the captain was in a better humor.

"You brought us luck, Padre," he said. "It was the fastest crossing I have made in two years."

"Then perhaps you will not mind taking us back again," said Kino.

The captain's smile faded. "How soon do you want to go? You know these ships always have to have some repairs made between voyages."

"Will a week be long enough?" asked Kino and, at the captain's reluctant nod, "Then we will visit the padres who have missions nearby and see how much food we can beg for the poor Indians of San Bruno." Kino and his young companion were back before the week was up. The mainland had suffered also from the drought. The priests of the Mexican missions were as generous as ever, but they had to consider their own native charges. All Padre Kino had been able to gather were five sheep in a pen, a few bags of corn. He looked at the captain, waiting with a small boat to take him out to the ship.

"Have you bought and loaded all the supplies the admiral ordered?" asked the padre.

"Prices are higher than ever," shrugged the captain. "Everything is aboard that I had money to pay for. And it does not look as if you had very good fortune, either, Padre Kino."

"We have permission to return north along the coast of the mainland," said Kino. "Perhaps the missions there have had more rain and can spare more food."

What he did not say was that he wanted to go north anyway, to see how far the Sea of California extended in that direction. The next morning, while the sheep *baaed* unhappily in their little pen on the pitching deck, Kino stood at the rail, pointing out to Hulo the way the mountains of Mexico sloped steeply into the sky from the very edge of the sea, the rocky canyons, the rivers shrunken to a trickle by the drought.

Hulo had picked up many Spanish words by this time, but he did not understand half the padre said. He could read Kino's face, however, and marked the disappointment in it when he could bring back only meager portions of wheat and a few squashes from the next mission when he was put ashore.

They went on to Tiburon Island, landed there for a brief exploration of its coast and to give Padre Kino a chance to get acquainted with the Seri Indians. He won their hearts and they begged him to stay with them, but the padre knew he must lose no further time in returning to his post in California.

Although they could see that the sea ran farther to the north, when they resumed their voyage the captain missed the narrow passage around the island. So they cruised across the sea to the west, went south along the coast of California and by August were once more at San Bruno.

It had rained while they were away. When Kino hurried ashore he found everything green.

"Look," he exulted, "even the doorposts sprout branches. And yet they call this country a desert!" But this could not change the fact that the long drought had been disastrous to the little colony. Fruit trees were dead. Gardens had been replanted, but they were not yet bearing. The Indians, hungrier than ever, had drifted away from the settlement. And to Kino's alarm, Admiral Atondo and his men were nowhere to be found. They might be diving for pearls farther down the coast, but he feared they had returned to the mainland. Padre Kino's orders were very clear. He must stay with the garrison, go where the admiral went. No padre would be allowed to remain here without military protection, no matter how eager he was to do so.

"We must go in search of them," he said to the captain. "South, to the Bay of La Paz, and if they are not there, then I shall have to return with you to Mexico." He turned to the bewildered Hulo. "This time you cannot go with me. God knows when we will return. I must leave you with your people."

As the ship weighed anchor, he stood at the rail, calling again and again, "I will come back!" But the weeping Hulo waded out until the water lapped his chin, holding out his arms, begging his beloved padre not to leave him.

His cries were still in Kino's ears that night as he lay sleepless on the deck, gazing up at the close bright stars. Ropes creaked in the rigging. The little ship smelled of tar and fish and the cattle, horses, and mules that had been its cargo on earlier voyages, as well as the poor sheep that still swayed in their pen. Kino noticed the smells no more than he did the hard, unyielding wooden deck beneath the saddle blanket he had thrown down for a bed. When a late moon drew a path of light across the water, the man at the wheel heard him murmuring and turned to see the padre on his knees, clenched hands raised heavenward, the glint of tears on his upturned face.

"He is praying to go back to that desert, to those Indians, that Hulo," said the man when the captain came to relieve him.

"He is crazy," scoffed the captain.

The other shook his head and crossed himself. "I do not think so. I think he is a saint."

Chapter 2

INDIANS SHALL NOT BE SLAVES!

[1685]

As a young man, Padre Eusebio Francisco Kino, like St. Francis Xavier, whose name he bore, had wished above all else to go as a missionary to China. The Jesuits had found favor at the Chinese court because of their mathematical learning and their map-making ability, so in all his years of study, the young Kino had worked hardest at mathematics. A brilliant student, he had been invited to become a professor in a great European university, but he was not even tempted to accept. His heart burned with one desire, to carry the Faith to China.

But as a Jesuit he had made a solemn vow to be obedient. When he was sent to Lower California instead, he went gladly, welcoming the hardships, asking only to bear them for the rest of his life. It almost broke his heart to leave the barren land and the people he had grown to love so much.

But leave them he must. When he found Admiral Atondo, a day's voyage south of San Bruno, the admiral, disappointed at the few pearls they had found, was ready to abandon his search and to sail to the mainland. And when they arrived Kino was ordered to report to his superior at the capital of Mexico.

Mexico City was not only the capital of New Spain, as Mexico was then called, it was also headquarters for the Jesuits. Set in a beautiful, fruitful valley, rimmed with snow-capped peaks, it was a pleasant place to live, a bustling, busy city of wide streets, great churches and the first university of this New World. A man of Padre Kino's brilliance and education should have been very happy there, but in his heart and mind were always the poor Indians of California. He tried one plan after another to get the mission re-established there. Each plan was considered, then rejected. It took too much money to ship supplies across the stormy sea.

But Kino was always full of hope. On the morning of June 19, 1686, he looked up with a smile as the door of his room swung wide and the Jesuit provincial entered.

But again the news was bad. "It would seem, Padre Kino," said the provincial, "we must give up the California mission at least for the present. I fear the Indians will soon forget all they know of Christianity."

"They will not forget!" cried Kino. "And I will not forget them. Wherever I go, I will gather provisions. Someday a mission will once again be established in California and when it is, we will supply it."

"A good idea," said the provincial, "and I am sending you to a place where you may be able to carry out your project."

Kino looked up eagerly. He had feared they would keep him here, to teach in the university. "Where?"

"Far to the northwest, to the most remote Spanish outpost of New Spain, in upper Sonora."

Kino beamed. No one had drawn any maps of that country. He would have a chance to explore, to find out for himself whether California was an island or a peninsula and whether or not an overland route could be found.

"God is good!" he said. "I will gather what is needed and leave as soon as possible."

He fingered a big blue abalone shell on the table. "I picked this up on the west coast of California," he said, turning it so the iridescent blue-green underside glowed in the light. "I will carry it with me always, as a reminder of the country to which I hope to return. I have been collecting shells for years and this one I have never found save on the shores of the Pacific."

Even for a man of action such as Padre Kino, it took much planning for a journey of fifteen hundred miles to establish a new mission. It was five long months before he was ready and mid-November when he set out. His mules were laden with bells, chalices and ornaments for the altar, along with enough supplies and equipment to last until he could begin to raise food for his own needs and those of his charges. As far as Guadalajara, the beautiful city in the mountains of western Mexico, he knew the road. He had been over it several times going to and coming from California. He had also visited coastal areas in the north, but although the road to Sonora paralleled the coast, it ran inland and there were few cities and towns along its course. He could expect hospitality only from scattered Jesuit missions and the Spanish mining camps.

He had some doubt about his reception at the latter. He carried with him a petition he had drawn up which, if granted, would stir up every mine owner in Mexico. Most of the mines were worked by Indian slaves. Padre Kino had learned that after the Jesuit padres had encouraged their converts to come to the settlements for instruction, the Spaniards seized them and made them work for nothing. As a result these Indians, being sensible men, decided that becoming a Christian meant becoming a slave. They stayed away from the settlements and the work of the missionaries was grinding to a halt.

It took a month to travel from Mexico City to Guadalajara. On the morning of December 16, 1686, Padre Kino rose to read his petition in the Royal Audiencia, or high court of justice, there. Word had gotten around that something of importance was about to happen and the room was crowded.

Briefly Kino stated the problem. The remedy, he said, was simple:

"Let no one be permitted to take, or cause any Indian to be taken for service until five years have passed after his conversion."

There was a hushed silence, then an angry murmur from behind him. The royal official made no move to take the petition. Was it to be refused? No, he was smiling.

"A royal order dealing with this very matter has just arrived from Spain," said the official. "The King and Queen have received complaints on this subject and wish it to be known throughout all the New World that no Indian shall be obliged to serve in the mines or work in any manner without pay for *twenty* years after baptism. Here is a copy of that order. You may take it with you."

He held out a scroll. Padre Kino, heart full to overflowing, took it and hurried away. Black looks followed him and there was more than one muttered, "Curse these meddling Jesuits!" from the ranks of the wealthy Spaniards who would always blame Kino for their loss of slave labor and stir up trouble against him at every opportunity.

He knew it and he did not care. His only thought was for the souls that awaited him. Perhaps in twenty years there would be other sources of labor for the mines. Perhaps the Spaniards would come to love the Indians as Kino did, treat them as brothers. At any rate, he would not have to worry about the problem of slavery for twenty blessed years.

He drove the pack train north at a grueling pace between the mountains and the sea, around canyons too steep to cross, fording rivers, carrying water from one dry camp to the next, working harder than anyone in the pack train. From one settlement to another they went, bringing news of the world, sending back letters to the provincial at the capital, and to a duchess in far-off Spain whom Kino had never met, but whose prayers and gifts had sustained him ever since he came to Mexico.

At night, beside the little fires, he thought of the long way he had come from the little town in the Tyrolese Alps of northern Italy where he was born in 1645. He forgot the disappointments and over and over again thanked God for the favors showered upon him. Then, after a thirst-provoking meal of sun-dried beef and equally dry tortillas, he rolled himself in a blanket and slept, to be up again before sunrise, helping with the packs, getting the mules lined out on the trail.

At the end of February, 1687, he reached Oposura in Sonora and reported to the Father Visitor, Padre Gonzalez. This time Kino watched as someone else sketched a map.

"Here is our last outpost," said Gonzalez, "at Cucurpe, on the San Miguel River. Beyond that point are the Pimas, a warlike, troublesome people."

He eyed the face of the newcomer. Kino's expression did

not change. His blue eyes eagerly scanned the rough map. "I had hoped to go to the Seri Indians on the Sea of California," he said, "but this is not too far away."

It was not the last time Padre Gonzalez would hear that word *California,* but now he paid little attention.

"Some of the Pimas threaten Spanish settlements," he said. "Do you think you can tame them?"

Kino smiled. "It will be easy, when they hear what has been done," and swiftly he told of the royal order.

"Twenty years!" exclaimed Gonzalez. "The mayor of Sonora must know of this at once."

And next day, at the capital city of San Juan, Kino had the pleasure of seeing the mayor read the royal paper, kiss it and place it above his head as a token of obedience not only for himself, but all the Spanish whom he represented.

Then Kino and Gonzalez were off to Cucurpe, Kino noting everything with his map-maker's eye. Cucurpe was near the western edge of mountain country. East of it was a series of rugged mountain chains, running from north to south, with

In February 1686, Father Manuel Gonzalez sends Kino to Pimería Alta in Sonora.

Spanish settlements in the valleys between. In the northeast the map was blank. That was Apache land and the Apache tribes were far worse than the Pimas, the scourge of Spanish and neighboring Indians alike.

"They ravage the border missions and outlying ranches," said Gonzalez. "They steal our horses and kill our cattle and inflict tortures on their captives. Worst of all, they keep even friendly tribes stirred up and ready for war. Soldiers try to patrol the country between the fort at San Juan and the one at Bacanuche, but it is difficult terrain."

Kino scarcely heard. His face was turned toward the Pimas. Although they had been pictured as warlike and troublesome, he had decided to wait and find out for himself. Sometimes Indians were troublesome because they had been badly treated.

Beyond Cucurpe, at a beautiful spot where the San Miguel River broke out of a canyon several hundred feet deep, Gonzalez said, "Here are your first charges," and pointed to a group of Indians outside a small village. Bordering it were rich bottom lands. The valley was ringed by mountain peaks. It was an ideal location for a mission, Kino thought, if the people would accept him.

"Chief Coxi asked us to send a priest," said Padre Gonzalez. "See? They wait for you," and indeed, the women and children were holding out their arms in welcome.

The chief was away, said one of the women, but a headman of the tribe was dying. Would they come and baptize him?

Ducking his head, Kino followed Gonzalez into the smoky gloom of the hut. These Indians were as dirty as the Californians, and smelled as bad, but they had asked for a priest. Surely the soul of this poor fellow would be taken swiftly to heaven.

Outside in fresher air, Gonzalez said, "There are other villages you may prefer to this one for your headquarters," but Kino shook his head. He felt as if he had come home. All that he lacked was a name for his mission. He thought for a moment, remembered a painting that had been given to him and rummaged through the packs for it.

"Nuestra Senora de los Dolores," he said proudly, using the Spanish name for Our Lady of Sorrows. And so the mission on the hill above the San Miguel River became known as Dolores. And it was well named for the Blessed Mother, for it would be the mother of many more missions.

Kino was so eager to begin his work that Padre Gonzalez was no sooner out of sight next morning than Kino said to the priest from Cucurpe, "Come, let us go to see some of the people in the neighboring villages." And together they rode westward across the mountain to visit the Pimas in the next valley. During the next three days they rode, and when they returned to Dolores, Kino wrote an enthusiastic letter to the Spanish duchess about the well-watered valleys, towering cottonwood trees, fertile fields and friendly natives. He had chosen sites for three more missions and named them San Ignacio, Imuris, and Remedios. Now he must begin to make adobe bricks for the church, instruct the people at Dolores, and baptize the children.

Easter came the last week in March that year and since Padre Kino could not celebrate it properly without a church, he was happy to accept the invitation to join his fellow missionaries at Tuape, farther down the river, where there was a spacious church. Although he had been at Dolores only two weeks, he took with him more than a hundred Pimas in a colorful procession down the valley.

Good-hearted Spanish ladies from a nearby mining town dressed the newly baptized Indian children in rich clothing and adorned them with their most beautiful jewels for the procession of the Blessed Sacrament. Were there muttered protests from their husbands, the mine owners? Did they say, "Baptized or not, Indians should be slaves?" If so, Padre Kino made no mention of it in his enthusiastic letter to the provincial.

But someone was not happy over his assignment to the Pimas. Even as the glorious Easter drew to a close, the pastor at Tuape took Kino aside and showed him a letter from Padre Gonzalez. It said that the mayor of Sonora, to whom Kino had shown the royal order prohibiting Indian slaves, had received a report that as soon as Kino arrived at Dolores, all the Pimas had moved away.

"Who would say such a thing?" cried Kino and, without waiting for an answer, "It does not matter who said it; the devil prompted it. We must let the Father Visitor know at once it is not true," and swiftly he penned a second letter to Gonzalez telling of the thirty children he had baptized, with two sons of Chief Coxi among them, of the number who came with him to Tuape, and that instead of moving away from Dolores, the Pimas were coming to live nearer the mission.

"Will you sign this with me?" he asked when he had finished, and both the pastor and a visiting Jesuit were glad to do so.

"He writes well," said the pastor next day as he watched Kino ride away at the head of his hundred Pimas.

"Well, and forcefully," agreed his visitor. "If it came to a fight, I think I would be very glad to have Padre Kino on my side."

Chapter 3

Among the Pimas

[1687]

Padre Kino had been at Dolores only about a month and a half when disturbing news came from a valley a hundred miles to the east. A ruthless Spanish officer had destroyed a whole Indian village and driven its inhabitants away. Condemned to death for his brutality, the officer escaped. Kino heard the Pimas talk about it. The white man was not punished, they said. He killed many innocent Indians and he was not punished. The soldiers let him run away.

Padre Kino shook his head sadly. That kind of wanton brutality could stir up a war of vengeance all along the border. That evening he went into the tiny church and stayed all night on his knees, face turned to heaven, asking God to bless these people, to help a humble padre save their souls, to permit him to work among them in peace.

Next day he found a heartening welcome at San Ignacio and Imuris and had almost forgotten about the Spanish officer as he rode beneath fragrant cottonwood trees toward

Remedios. He intended to spend the night there, and return the next day to Dolores. But what was this? The village looked deserted.

Kino turned in the saddle and motioned to Francisco, the interpreter.

"Where are the people?"

Francisco shrugged. "I do not know. I will see if I can find them."

A little later Kino sat in front of the headman's hut and looked at the surly group rounded up by Francisco. At first they would say nothing. Then one of them spat out a few angry words.

"They do not want you here," said the interpreter. "They do not want to be Christian."

"Why?" said Kino.

"They say they do not want their village destroyed."

So, thought Kino, the people of Remedios have heard about the wicked soldier. He was a white man, so was Kino, therefore not to be trusted—that was the way they reasoned.

Two of the men began to talk at once. Presently Francisco turned back to Kino. "Even if you do not destroy their village, you will make them work so hard for the Church they will have no time to plant their crops. And you pasture so many cattle the watering places dry up. That is what these people say."

Once again the first man spoke and this time Kino understood the words. He had heard them many times before, and it was easy to see why the Indians believed them.

"The padres kill people with their holy oils," said the man and Kino remembered a dying woman he had baptized and anointed in the last rites when he was here on his first trip.

"None of the things they say are true," Kino began slowly,

using some of the Pima words he had learned.

"You lie to the Indians!" interrupted the man angrily and, to Francisco, "This padre said he had a paper from the King to protect the Indians. If he had such a paper he would show it to the soldiers at Bacanuche."

Swiftly Francisco translated and Kino threw up his hands. No use talking to people who felt like this. It had not been enough to show the royal order at San Juan two months ago. He would have to take it to the fort at Bacanuche also.

"We do not stay here tonight," he said. "We will return to Dolores."

That evening, almost before the packs were off the mules, Padre Kino was giving orders for another ride. The next day he took Chief Coxi with him to Bacanuche, with other Indian officials, and all of them were present when Kino talked to the lieutenant at the fort. The officer was friendly, the reception more than cordial. There were Spanish mines near the settlement and Kino made sure their owners knew what was in the royal order. Then, hoping he had proved his good faith and honesty to the Indians, he went back to Dolores and settled down to work.

If the people of Remedios did not care to become Christians, they were in the minority. Indians began moving to Dolores from the country for miles around. By the end of June, 1687, Padre Kino had baptized sixty babies and several adults. His Indians had learned to chant the prayers, the Creed, and the Gloria, and they could say the Act of Contrition as well as those who had known it for years.

During the first months at Dolores, Kino managed to build a small church. The Pimas loved the holy pictures, the beautiful things on the altar, the small chiming bells. Now larger bells arrived from the capital of Mexico and the people listened with delight when they were rung.

It was no surprise when Chief Coxi came with his wife one day to ask for baptism, but Padre Kino was greatly pleased. Coxi was an important man among the Pimas. He was not only chief of this village, but of other tribes living between here and the Sea of California. His reception into the Church must be a solemn occasion and Kino planned it carefully.

He made the chief wait for a month, until July 31. Then not only Coxi and his wife were baptized, but forty Indians with them. Spanish gentlemen came from Bacanuche to sponsor the new Christians and the padre from Cucurpe brought his whole choir. There were solemn vespers, a sung Mass, a procession. The Pimas loved it. Five chiefs from principal villages in the north and west came afterward to Kino and asked that padres be sent to them, too.

Were there mine owners among the Spanish from Bacanuche? If so, Kino welcomed them along with the rest, perhaps hoping they would consider their religion a little more and their pocketbooks less when they thought of Christian Indians in the future.

Kino now had more converts than he could care for and he sent letters to his Jesuit friends asking for anything they could send him. They responded generously, and six months later he wrote to one of them that he had been able to wash three hundred Indians in the water of baptism and that five thousand more had come asking to receive the sacrament.

It was not altogether piety that brought them. Everyone who came was fed. The other missions had contributed cattle, sheep, goats, and orchard trees when Padre Kino came to Dolores. The Pimas were natural farmers, some of them even using elaborate systems of irrigation in their fields.

Kino introduced new foods and taught them to increase the yield of their crops many times over. Word spread all over the country that there was always food at Dolores. Other Pimas envied those under Kino's care and begged him to come and help them, too.

In January of 1689, Padre Gonzalez had heard so many splendid reports of Kino's work that he came on a tour of inspection. Kino sent word through Chief Coxi to the adjacent villages and many Pimas came to see the strange Black Robe as he rode with Kino around the little quadrangle of Indian villages and back to Dolores again.

Kino told Padre Gonzalez that he had questioned the Indians and what they said made him eager to explore new country to the north. First, however, he had to make sure that Dolores was solidly established. And while he was doing that, he begged that other priests be sent to the region. Baptisms could be numbered in the thousands if there were priests to instruct the people.

It was a big country and the missions were far apart. Many of the padres suffered from loneliness. Padre Kino kept so busy he did not let himself think of his lack of congenial companions, but even he was delighted when Padre Juan Salvatierra came traveling through the region, sent by the Jesuit provincial on a tour of inspection of the missions in the north. He arrived at Dolores on Christmas Eve, 1689. Kino took one look at the square-jawed, hawk-nosed, weather-beaten face and knew that here was a man he was going to like. The new church was not yet finished, but a joyous Nativity season was celebrated in it just the same.

Like Kino, Salvatierra was a learned man and a fearless explorer. He had come from the war-torn mountains where two Jesuits had been martyred. Stories from this Pima country made him think the same troubles might be brewing here. In fact, the provincial had asked him to look into them. He was therefore puzzled by the cordial reception he received from the Pimas at Dolores. And when he and Kino rode out to the missions, accompanied by Chief Coxi, he was amazed and delighted to see the amount of building that Kino had been able to do in less than three years.

At Remedios the Indians were still sullen and uncooperative, but at Imuris and San Ignacio, the Black Robes were welcomed by crowds of friendly natives. And as they traveled northward to visit four new missions it was a triumphal procession, with smiling natives lined up to greet the padres at every village. Far up the Altar River, in what is now Arizona, seven hundred Indians awaited the visitors, knelt before them, and begged them to visit their village.

Who could resist such an appeal? The padres went on to the north, crossed a divide and descended to the Santa Cruz River where they found prepared for them three brush shelters, one in which to say Mass, another where they were to sleep, a third for use as a kitchen. There were more than forty houses in the village and Salvatierra was so impressed by the size of the place and the attitude of the Indians he promised to send a priest to this place as soon as he could.

That evening he and Kino sat in the brush shelter and looked out at the distant mountains. The pleasant smell of burning pinon came from smoke from the cooking fires curling into the dark blue sky of evening.

Salvatierra had been examining the houses. They were built of upright ribs that looked like sunflower stalks, bound together with material from the giant cactus called *sahuaro,* then plastered with mud mixed with straw.

"They are roughly made," he said, "but they keep out the cold." Then he said slowly, "I must confess that when I came to Dolores I was troubled. There were many conflicting reports. Some said that priests were not needed, that there are few Indians in Pima country. Still another story which came to the ears of our provincial was that the Pima Indians are so stupid they cannot learn, so it is useless to send missionaries to them."

"You have seen that such stories are lies," said Kino.

"They were lies," said Salvatierra.

Just then there were shouts from the edge of the village and Chief Coxi hurried toward them. "Warriors come from the north," he said excitedly. "Come and see!"

The two followed him and came face to face with a band of Indians with painted faces, wearing brightly colored feathers, beads and blankets. They had lances in their hands, but they were far from warlike. When they saw the Black Robes, they fell on their knees.

"They wish you to come and visit them," said Chief Coxi. "They come from a great town to the north called Bac. By comparison this is a small village."

Kino looked at Salvatierra. Regretfully the Father Visitor shook his head. "We cannot go. I have already been away too long."

"But I will come this way again," said Kino, using some of his newly acquired Pima words. "I will come to visit you at Bac." It was a solemn promise.

They turned south the next morning, riding through fine bottom lands and cottonwood groves that lined the sparkling Santa Cruz River. At Santa Maria, near the crest of the divide, they stayed to baptize babies and instruct their parents, then packed up their vestments and portable altar, and were off to Dolores, stopping at two other places along the way. They had traveled more than two hundred miles through beautiful country, among pleasant, welcoming people. If Salvatierra had had any doubts that Pima land needed more missionaries he had them no longer.

"I have never seen a more pleasant people, a more productive country," he exclaimed to Padre Kino as they rode along.

Kino's eyes glowed. "They are so indeed! And do you know what has long been the wish of my heart. It is to grow enough grain and raise enough cattle in this Pima country to supply the poor people of California."

Salvatierra looked at him thoughtfully. Ever since they left Dolores, Kino had come back constantly to the subject of California and the natives he had had to abandon there. Although he had done so much good since, he seemed unable to forget them. He was very persuasive. From what Padre Kino said those missions should be re-established. Padre Salvatierra thought he would like to be the man to do it, but he knew the difficulties and did not like to raise false hopes. So he said nothing more.

As the friendly Salvatierra rode away from Dolores, Kino wondered how much the talk of California had meant to him, if he would really try to go there. Kino would not know for a long time. Shortly after Salvatierra's return from the expedition, he was appointed rector of the Jesuit College at Guadalajara. Once more California would have to wait.

During the next busy year, Kino recalled his promise to visit the Pimas at Bac, but time after time something occurred to prevent his going to them. When he heard that Indians in that area had gone on a rampage and stolen a herd of horses from one of the missions, he feared he might be too late. The soldiers sent out to find and punish the thieves might massacre innocent Indians instead, perhaps even those of Bac. But the officer in charge this time was a level-headed fellow. He found the guilty ones, made peace with them and brought a band of their chiefs to Dolores. They had heard of the black-robed Kino and when they saw him they begged that a padre be sent to them.

After they had gone, Kino thought, "One soldier treats the Indians like wild beasts and all who hear of it become suspicious and angry. Another officer considers them his native brothers, with souls like his own, and as a result we can bring the Faith to their whole tribe and their neighbors."

But not everyone shared his pleasure in what had been accomplished. About this time two mine owners met in Bacanuche. One of them said, "What do you think of Padre Kino?"

"He is a wall of brass against us!" cried the other. "Until he came we had almost convinced the governor that the Pimas were rebels and enemies and should be given to us as slaves, for the good of the country. Now look what has happened! This Kino has baptized hundreds of them and built heaven knows how many new churches. We must do something about him, and soon!"

His companion laughed shortly. "You will say nothing against Kino to the governor. Do you realize that for the first time since the Spanish came to Sonora, there is peace among the Pimas? I need slaves as badly as you do, but we will not risk an Indian uprising to get them. No, *mi amigo,* we will not interfere with Padre Kino. His friends are too powerful."

Chapter 4

THE YOUNG LIEUTENANT

[1694]

In December, 1693, Padre Kino set forth on a first brief visit to the Pima Indians of the Lower Altar Valley. These people were called the Sobas. Their chief was known as the great El Soba. In this unexplored country Kino found natives who were gentle and affable despite their fright at the white faces they had never seen before. The padre saw a great field for missionary work among them, but he needed time and official cooperation to prepare a second expedition down the Altar River to the Sea of California.

So he went to San Juan to ask the officer in command, General Jironza, to assign someone to travel with him as a representative of the Spanish government. The general agreed and decided that his own nephew, young Lieutenant Manje, should accompany Padre Kino.

On the first day of February, 1694, Kino, black robe tucked up around his knees, bustled about the plaza at San Juan, shouting orders to his muleteers and urging them to finish their packing. As Jironza stood watching the preparations, young Manje strode across the plaza. In his hand were several light canes with multicolored ribbons fluttering from them.

"See, my uncle," he said proudly, "do these look important enough?"

Padre Kino hurried over. "We are almost ready, Lieutenant." And, with a look at the beribboned canes, "What are those?"

General Jironza said, "My nephew will distribute these canes to the chiefs of the villages, as symbols of authority, granted by the civil and military government of Spain."

Kino's eyes twinkled. "They will please the chiefs, you may be sure. Let us see how Coxi responds to such a gift," and he beckoned to the chief who stood beside some saddled horses. Coxi strutted toward them, a beaming smile on his brown face as Kino made a solemn speech in Pima language, then indicated to Manje with a nudge that he was to present the cane.

Chief Coxi received his beribboned cane of office from young Lieutenant Manje. Coxi bowed, took it, waved delightedly to his watching friends and marched proudly back to his horses, holding the cane stiffly before him.

Manje laughed and turned to embrace the general. "Adios, my dear uncle. We will count all the Indians from here to the Sea and tell them they are to be your loyal subjects."

"I wish I could go with you." General Jironza looked up at the blue sky, where towering white clouds sailed eastward above the mountains. It was a beautiful time of year to travel and Padre Kino was an excellent companion. The general felt he was doing his nephew a favor by sending him along.

Lieutenant Manje had not been away from Spain very long; he was young, and everything in this new country interested him. He wanted to know about deposits of gold and silver, why the canyons all ran from north to south and then all at once turned west, what kind of crops grew in the valleys and the name of each river and stream they crossed. His three-day ride to Dolores with Father Kino was a pleasant one and at the mission no time was lost in assembling supplies for the extended trip to the west.

"This is where we are going," Father Kino said to Manje, tracing a map on the hard-packed earth of the plaza at Dolores. "We will cross over a low mountain pass to the west, and follow the San Ignacio River until it joins the Altar."

Lieutenant Manje nodded. This river flowed south like the others, and then turned west. He watched as Kino showed how the Altar Valley came in from the north. Below the place where the rivers met was a town, he said, and lettered in the name, *Caborca*.

"I was there last December," said Kino. "There are many Pimas in that country, but two tribes keep fighting each other. Chief Soba is the warlike one. I hope on this expedition to meet him and persuade him to keep the peace. Then, perhaps, we can send a missionary to Caborca. It is a fine place for a mission. And it is very close to the Sea of California."

The next morning, riding west at the head of the pack train, Kino spoke again of California. "The poor Indians there," he said, "have never seen such fields as the ones around Dolores. It is my plan to gather food among these missions, to pasture many cattle and sheep, to let the herds and flocks increase, so that when the missions of California are once more established, we can send supplies to them."

"The Indians of California, are they Pimas, too?" asked Manje.

"No, they are entirely different tribes."

"They speak a different language?" persisted Manje.

"Yes."

"Will Pimas share their food supplies with strangers?" Manje asked bluntly.

Kino looked surprised. "Of course they will. The Pimas are a friendly, generous people."

Manje looked at him doubtfully. Most of the young lieutenant's experience with Indians had been obtained by riding with his uncle's Flying Column against the Apaches. Even the flying hoofs of the mounted troops were seldom fast enough to catch the marauders who swooped down on small settlements to plunder, kill, and burn. Manje had begun to think of all the Indians of this new world as cruel savages. The Pimas at Dolores were a busy, happy group, but were all Pimas like that? Lieutenant Manje doubted it.

Padre Kino seemed to know how to handle them. He spoke in their own language and Manje marveled at how much they seemed to understand. It must sound like a strange story, he

Kino and Manje

thought, leaning against a tall cottonwood tree the first night at Caborca and watching the intent brown faces upturned to Kino as he preached to them. What could they know of God and His Holy Law, and how did the padre find words in the Pima language to express such things? When he spoke of the burning fires of hell, the Indians showed their horror. When he turned to description of rewards in heaven, Manje was amused to see their eyes turn to the cane with its bright ribbons which he had presented to their chief this afternoon.

"How do you know what to say?" he asked curiously the next morning as Kino rode west beside him toward the spot near the coast from which the padre had promised his young companion a view of the mountains of California.

Kino said, "It is not hard to tell about God and His Laws."

"In the Pima language?"

"Yes, even in Pima," said Kino. "When I first came to Dolores, one of the padres sent me a blind Indian who could speak Spanish and Pima as well. I learned from him how to begin. And, of course, you know Francisco, the interpreter who goes with me."

He was gazing ahead to the steep slopes of a mountain from the top of which he hoped to look again across the sea. "It was much harder in California. There we had to learn each word as we went along. It will be easier for the next padre who goes there, because we made a long list of words in Spanish and the California Indian language."

Again he talked of California and when they climbed the mountain, Lieutenant Manje was thrilled as he looked out at the magnificent view before them. It was as the padre had said: the Sea was not wide at this point and beyond the blue waters of the gulf the towering peaks of California were clearly visible.

As they jumped and slid back down the steep slopes to the place where they had left the horses, Kino was full of enthusiastic plans to cross the sand dunes on the following day and go to the very edge of the Sea. Perhaps he would find new shells to add to his collection.

"I saw a big blue shell on your table at Dolores," said Manje. "Perhaps we will find more like it tomorrow. I would like one to take to my uncle."

Kino shook his head. "It is an abalone shell from the ocean to the west of California. When I was there we searched the beaches all along the eastern side of the island and found many beautiful shells, but no big blue ones like that. I think we will find none tomorrow, either."

And he was right. The next morning they went on foot across the remaining six miles to the Sea, sniffed the fresh salt air and congratulated each other that their expedition would go down in history, for they were the first to reach this shore in the sixty years since Sonora had been settled. Although they picked up plenty of seashells, there were no big blue ones. Now Padre Kino would treasure the one he had more than ever. He doubted that he would find another unless he again crossed California to the Pacific Ocean.

"Do you know what the provincial writes to me from Mexico City?" Kino asked Manje as they turned back toward Caborca. "He would like to have me build a boat, carry it in pieces with oxen and mules to the Sea and put it together there, so we may explore around the top of the Island of California."

Manje laughed. It sounded like a wild idea, but he was beginning to think this Padre Kino could do anything he set his mind to. And his Pimas would help him!

Manje looked at the irrigated fields and the fertile lands around Caborca. The people grew corn, beans and melons. There was fine pasture land and much timber.

"If they had axes," Manje said, "they could clear enough land here to support three thousand Indians. And it is a temperate climate." Kino was right in thinking it an ideal place for a mission. But what about the warlike Chief Soba, who lived nearby?

He had his answer the day they left Caborca and were met by forty of Soba's men and the chief himself. All were unarmed, all were naked. So this was the great Soba! Truly you could not believe anything you heard in this country!

The chief had come to tell Kino he wished to be his friend. Beaming, Kino presented him with a pack-load of meal, only to find that the Indians had no container for it. At last Chief Soba commanded his wife and another woman to take off the deerskins which they wore. The poor women hid in a clump of bushes while the meal was poured into the skins, then the chief had his men gather it up and they all went off together, while Manje laughed until he had to hold onto his saddle horn to keep from falling off. What a story this was to tell his uncle!

The letter, when he sat down to write it after they had returned to Dolores, contained more than a funny story. True to his promise, young Manje had been counting Indians, nine hundred and fifty of them. Padre Kino had baptized fifty children and a few adults who were gravely ill. Others had been instructed in the Holy Faith and the whole area was now at peace. Manje could scarcely wait to get back to it.

At Dolores, Kino assembled his Indian carpenters and began to make ribs and timbers for the boat. The keel and mast would have to be fashioned from the fine trees at Caborca. It did not bother the padre that none of his workmen had ever built a boat before. From somewhere he produced plans. He was justifying the lieutenant's confidence that he could do whatever needed to be done.

By the middle of March he was back at Caborca, and Lieutenant Manje with him. The lieutenant wanted to set out at once to explore the country to the south and west, but Kino needed all hands to fell the tall, thick cottonwood tree he had chosen for the boat and it was up to Manje to wield an axe with the rest.

They dug around the base of the tree, chopping off roots as they came to them. The taproot, however, went straight down and try as they might, they could not get at it. The tree refused to fall.

"I'll climb it," Manje said at last. "I will go up and tie a rope near the top, climb down again, and let the Indians pull it over." Before anyone could stop him he swarmed up into the leafy branches. The tree swayed with his weight, but he kept on, pulling the rope after him as he stepped from one big branch to the next. Just as he looped the end around the trunk one of the Indians yelled and Manje felt the tree start to topple, slowly at first, then with a swift rush of crashing branches as the taproot popped and let go. It was a good thing the limbs were big and leafy. They cushioned the fall enough to let Manje jump free and land on his feet, shaken, but without a scratch. The Indians laughed and applauded, as if he had done it on purpose, but Padre Kino went off by himself, sank down on his knees and thanked God for preserving the life of the rash young fellow to whom he had already become devoted.

When the tree was trimmed and ready for shaping, Manje took off with a few men and supplies enough to last several days. When he returned he found Kino ready to leave. The wood had to season, Kino said, before they could go on with the boat. So the pack train returned to Dolores.

By June, Kino judged that the timbers were sufficiently seasoned and took off with Manje on a third expedition to Caborca. There had been Indian thefts and raids all up and down the border. It was said that some of the Pimas had taken part in them. Kino decided to take a little different route from Dolores this time—through Tubutama on the upper Altar River.

The priest there had a gory tale to tell. Kino shook his head as he listened.

"This Lieutenant Solis who came here with the Flying Column," he interrupted before the priest had finished, "is it the same Solis who went to look for stolen horses in Arizona, earlier this year?"

The construction of the boat in the desert.

"There is only one Lieutenant Solis," said Manje.

"Do you know what he did?" cried Kino. "He found racks of drying meat at a small village near Bac. His troops came down upon the people so swiftly they ran away. He hunted them down like wild animals and killed two of them. Then his soldiers discovered that the meat was venison, that the people of that village knew nothing of the stolen horses. It was a dreadful thing. The Pimas were not to blame. And you sent for this Solis to come here, Padre?"

"I sent to the fort for help." Unhappily the priest went on with his story. "My life was in danger. There were two troublemakers who kept saying bad things against me and stirring up all the Indians."

"What did Solis do?" asked Manje.

"Arrested the two men, let me baptize them and listen to their confessions and then hanged them."

"And since then?" prompted Manje.

"Everything is quiet." The padre of Tubutama looked at Kino. "What else could I do? I am here alone in this great Altar Valley. The nearest mission is over a hundred miles away."

Again Kino shook his head. "Lieutenant Solis knows no other way to deal with Indians but to kill them."

Lieutenant Manje frowned. He did not admire Lieutenant Solis, but he considered him a brave soldier—and after you saw a few Apache massacres, you could understand the desire for revenge.

As the priest had said, all was quiet at Tubutama, so the next morning Padre Kino hurried down the river toward Caborca, while Lieutenant Manje went off on a journey of exploration to the northwest. He had replenished his supply of official canes and Kino furnished him with gifts and provisions. Francisco, the interpreter, went with the young man and the first night, at a village of four hundred inhabitants, Manje talked of God and His Law, as well as of obedience to the Spanish authorities. He concluded the lecture by presenting a beribboned cane and the chief in this place was as pleased as Coxi had been.

The next village was a disappointment, with poverty-stricken people whose only water supply was a pool green with slime. The Indians went about naked and lived in the middle of a dry, sterile plain. They had so little to eat Manje gave them all the provisions he could spare. In return for his kindness, they warned him not to go any farther north, that a tribe of cannibals lived in great houses beside a big river.

Manje's guides, more and more frightened the farther they went from familiar territory, now insisted on turning back to the south again. But the venturesome Manje would not go the way they had come. He headed southwest through country so dry and forbidding they had to travel over eighty miles in one day before they found a water supply. It was not very good water, either, but they drank it. . . . And the next day Manje reeled into Caborca, burning with fever.

Padre Kino had been awaiting his arrival with some impatience, intending to leave for Dolores as soon as Manje joined him. Kino had received some bad news. The new Father Visitor thought it impossible to build a boat this far from the Sea and transport it overland to water. He had sent word to stop work on it at once!

One look at the young lieutenant's crimson face and Kino gave orders to unpack. For the next four days the fever raged. One night Manje was so gravely ill the padre thought he would not live until morning and administered the last sacraments.

"Take me out of this burning hot country!" begged Manje, rallying a little. So the next morning, they started up the river toward Dolores, the Indians carrying the sick man on their shoulders part of the way and holding him in the saddle when they could, to make better time. For six desperate days they traveled thus, covering only a little over a hundred miles in that period, the lieutenant delirious, unable to swallow more than a mouthful of gruel now and then.

At the mission of San Ignacio, Padre Campos, the Jesuit now in charge, came out to meet them. He took a look at the patient and urged Kino to leave him there.

"I know how to treat a fever," said Campos. "The patient is not allowed to drink water, not so much as a drop!"

So Kino went on to Dolores and Lieutenant Manje tossed from side to side on his hard bed, feeling somewhat better, but wildly thirsty. One night he lay there gazing up at the water jar which Campos had put on a high shelf, far out of his reach. He would reach it; he must! Inch by inch he dragged himself up, almost fainting with weakness, but just as he reached the shelf the jar tipped and cold water drenched him from head to foot. The jar crashed to the floor and Manje yelled. Campos stumbled sleepily into the room, scolding as he came. "You will kill yourself. You must not have the cold water. Get back in bed—no, wait! I must give you some dry clothing."

Manje subsided, muttering, as thirsty as when he had made his try for the water, for not so much as a drop of it had gone down his throat. But something, perhaps the shock of the drenching, broke the fever. He woke next morning with a clear head, asked for food and within nine days was hurrying on to Dolores to inform Padre Kino that he had entirely recovered.

"You may think you are well." Kino put his arm around the young man's shoulders. "I think you must rest for a while. Go back to your uncle at San Juan. I am going to Bac, and north to the great houses you were told about."

Manje grinned. "I thought you did not believe my story, that you thought I had imagined the whole thing."

"So you remember what you said while you had the fever? Well, since then I have had visitors from the north. They too spoke of the great houses."

"And did they tell you the people there are cannibals?"

Kino smiled. "When I came to Dolores, they told me all Pimas were cannibals. If I believed half the things I hear about places I want to visit, I would never leave Dolores. But when I go in spite of the stories, all along the way I find friendly people, eager to hear about God. So it will be this time. You will see."

At San Juan, Manje repeated the conversation to his uncle and General Jironza said with a troubled frown, "Do you think we should send soldiers with Padre Kino? We must not let anything happen to him."

"No." Lieutenant Manje scratched his head ruefully. Due to the fever, no doubt, his hair was coming out in handfuls. "No," he said again, "something may happen to others who go with him, but not to Padre Kino. I think God will not let anything bad happen to him—ever! He is one of the bravest men I ever knew and I have learned much from him that is for the good of Spain. I have put all these things down in my report to you, my uncle, and I thank you for letting me accompany him on those expeditions."

Chapter 5

Blood of a Martyr

[1694]

Shortly after Kino's return from Caborca to Dolores, he made a journey north to Bac and beyond, to the Gila River, to see "the great houses." They proved to be amazing ruins of an earlier civilization, but Padre Kino was not as impressed by them as he was by the friendly Pimas who welcomed him wherever he went. Accompanied only by natives on this journey, he went back to Dolores in the firm belief that a padre could go anywhere in Pima country in perfect safety.

At Dolores he found that his request had been granted to establish a mission at Caborca and a priest was being sent there. In October, 1694, young Padre Saeta arrived at Dolores and Kino began at once to assemble supplies for him.

On the morning of October 19, Chief Coxi's young son hauled a heavily laden pack over the dusty plaza toward his father, crying, "Where do we go? And why is Padre Kino so happy?"

"We go on a journey to the west, to Caborca again," said the chief. "Padre Kino is always happy when we prepare for a journey."

"But look," the youngster waved toward the black-robed padres watching a band of mares in a corral. Kino, his own dusty garment hiked up as usual about his knees, waved both arms as he shouted instructions to the Indian herdsmen. "What does he do with those horses?" persisted the boy.

"The horses and cattle and sheep and goats and mules and much wheat and corn he gives to the young padre to start a mission," said Chief Coxi proudly. After all, these animals had thrived under his care, these grains had been grown in the fields around Dolores. It was his gift as well as Kino's.

"Why does he give away so much?"

"All padres share what they have," said another voice as Francisco, the interpreter, stopped to look over the pack animals. "Are you ready, Chief Coxi?" he asked. "Padre Kino wishes to start as early as we can. There will be many stops along the way, so people may see the new Padre Saeta."

Chief Coxi picked up the reins that trailed from his horse's bridle and threw himself across its back. His son jumped on a box and from it to his own horse. Kino and the new padre had saddles, but most of the Indians rode bareback, or with a blanket cinched on the horse's back. For a people who had known horses only since the Spaniards brought them into the country, the Pimas were excellent riders. So were the warlike Apaches, unfortunately. Apaches were always stealing horses, and Pimas always getting blamed for it.

Chief Coxi spat into the dust and reined his mount around to look back at the bawling cattle, sheep *baa-baaing* in their wake and village dogs yapping at their heels. It was fine stock they were giving the new padre.

Kino too was thinking of the stock as he rode along. He glanced at the handsome young Padre Saeta and hoped the animals would thrive under his care.

His heart was light as they rode along. Everything was going as he had prayed it would. Only two days before, the Father Visitor had left Dolores for the north with another new padre who, by now, was installed at Cocóspora. That made seven priests in the district of Dolores. This Saeta who rode beside him would make eight. Kino hoped all of them would stay.

"You may be able to plant a field of wheat right away," said Kino. "One good shower of rain in November and you will have a fine crop the following May."

"Only one rain during the winter?" asked Saeta.

"There may be more, but even if there is not, you will always find water in the sand. At Caborca, water flows the year round at some places in the river bed. In the packs are small trees for your orchard—peach, pomegranate, and lemon trees. At San Ignacio walnuts do well, but I do not know whether they will grow at Caborca. Oranges should, however. If I go to the City of Mexico next year I will try to bring back some orange trees."

He turned to look back, but the horses were traveling at a good pace and all he could see were clouds of dust. He began to talk again of this wonderful Pima country, how the Indians here were raising corn, wheat, beans, melons, and squashes when he came. He called the latter calabashes and said they were so common the Indians said, "Eat calabash," when they meant having a meal of any kind.

Saeta listened and tried to remember everything. He was as pleased to be here as Kino was delighted to have him.

"What about wild fruit?" he asked eagerly. "In the south the Indians eat delicious fruit from a cactus. They call it *pitahaya.* Does it grow near Caborca?"

"There may be some, I do not know. The fruit of the giant *sahuaro* cactus is also good. And do you know the vegetable called *bledo?* It grows wild on the flats along the river. When it is young and tender it is better than asparagus. Even after it grows up the cattle eat it. There will be plenty of forage around your mission, Padre."

It took a great deal of food for the small army of Indians who assembled to build the church at Caborca. Within a week after Kino left, Saeta wrote that they had made five hundred adobe bricks. They were proud to think of having their own church, their own padre, and whole families moved into Caborca to help with the work—and share in the rewards for working. Padre Saeta soon discovered he would have to have help to feed them all and went off on an expedition to other missions, begging for corn, wheat and beef. His people were quarrying stone, cutting timbers and putting them in place. Men who work like that must be fed, and well fed.

Kino added sixty additional head of cattle, sixty sheep and goats to what Dolores had already given and sent with them a quantity of wheat and corn. Saeta had equally good luck wherever he went, due partly to the generosity of his fellow Jesuits, partly to his enthusiasm and engaging personality. Everybody liked him. Everybody was glad to help him.

He had been at Caborca almost four months when early in March, 1695, Padre Kino, no doubt remembering the kindness of his neighboring pastors during his first Holy Week in Pimaland, wrote to ask Saeta to come to Dolores for Easter. The young padre replied that he was too busy. "I am building a town, growing crops, and enclosing pastures for my stock," he wrote. "Later, perhaps we may meet midway at Magdalena."

The letter was written on Good Friday, April 1. Before Kino received it, a rash of Indian troubles erupted in Pima country, starting at Tubutama, where Lieutenant Solis had hanged the two troublemakers the year before.

It had been quiet since at Tubutama, but not peaceful. The padre there, invited to Dolores for Easter, had no sooner left Tubutama on March 29 when one of his Indian foremen from another tribe abused a Pima workman. He yelled for help. Other Pimas came with arrows and killed the foreman, along with two of his friends. That roused the whole village and before the day was over they had set fire to the mission house and church, desecrated sacred articles from the altar and killed the mission cattle.

Padre Campos heard of the trouble at San Ignacio. The priest from Tubutama had not arrived and Campos was sure he had been killed. Campos started out with some of his Indians, hoping to rescue him and the two padres met on the road. There was no question of going back. Together they hurried toward Dolores and the meeting with their fellow Jesuits for Easter.

The Tubutama Indians, angry at their padre's escape, turned their faces toward the new mission downriver, at Caborca. They arrived at Padre Saeta's door very early on the morning of Holy Saturday and although he had heard of trouble at another mission, he seemed to have no fear of these strange Indians, but invited them into the house and talked to them for a while. On their way out he took them through the hall which he was using as a church. In the yard they turned on him, drew their bows, notched their arrows. Saeta fell to his knees and spread his arms wide. Two arrows pierced his body. He rose, ran to his room, picked up a crucifix and kissed it, then fell across his bed while his murderers shot a shower of arrows into his body.

His assistants were the next victims. Francisco, the interpreter from Dolores, and two more Indians from that mission reddened the sand with their blood. Then, as they had done at Tubutama, the Indians set fire to the house, destroyed the altar, defiled the sacred vessels and either killed or drove away all the cattle, sheep, goats and horses they could find.

Easter Sunday was drawing to a close when a faithful Caborca Indian staggered into the plaza at Dolores. He had brought his frightful news almost a hundred and fifty

The martyrdom of Father Saeta in Caborca Sonora.

miles in twenty-seven hours. Shortly after his arrival, another messenger brought the Good Friday letter from the martyred Saeta. Then messages began to come to Padre Kino from everywhere: the east, where the Apaches threatened, the southeast, where rebellion flared again. If revolt spread among the Pimas, every mission in Sonora might be wiped out, as the Franciscan missions had been destroyed in New Mexico eighteen years before.

Kino sent an urgent plea for help to General Jironza and dispatched Chief Felipe, an Indian governor, to Caborca to find out exactly what had happened. Jironza got together a mixed force of soldiers and Indian warriors, and, joined by Lieutenant Manje and two priests, headed for Tubutama.

The village was deserted. They turned south along the Altar River. Before they reached Caborca, they met Chief Felipe on his way to Dolores, to report to Padre Kino. According to custom in this hot country, he had burned the bodies of those who had been killed. He had brought the crucifix which Padre Saeta embraced as he was dying. Felipe knelt on the ground, bowed his head, and held out the crucifix to the general.

Jironza was a hardened soldier, but the sight of this precious relic brought tears to his eyes. He took it reverently and exclaimed at the beauty of the workmanship.

Lieutenant Manje was not looking at the crucifix, but at the horizon, where a swarm of black-winged dots circled cloudlike above a certain spot in the west.

"Let me go ahead and reconnoiter, my uncle," he said. "I know the country." At Jironza's nod, he beckoned to his bodyguard and rode on.

As Manje and his escort rode into Caborca the hush of death was broken only by the thunder of an arquebus which Manje ordered fired to drive away the circling vultures. They did not disperse, but swooped down a little farther distant on carcasses of dead cattle, killed by the raiding Indians and left to rot in the hot spring sun.

Jironza rode up with the others. Caborca was deserted. Even innocent Indians stayed at a safe distance in the hills when soldiers came on a mission such as this.

Jironza and Manje gathered up the bones and ashes of the dead Saeta, placed them in a box and locked it. From the shambles that had been his room, they picked up twenty-two arrows. The soldiers searched for vestments, books, missals, any sacred vessels that might have been overlooked. Everything of value was gone, the roofless buildings empty, open to the sky.

General Jironza looked grimly at the fields along the river. Padre Saeta had obeyed Kino's injuction to plant wheat in November. It was a magnificent crop, heavy yellowing heads rippling in the warm breeze, standing almost tall enough to hide a man.

"Destroy it!" said the general harshly. "Do not leave one grain to feed the murderers!"

Swiftly his men obeyed, cutting the grain, then turning three hundred horses into the fields. The corn, not yet ripe, suffered the same fate. When the soldiers moved away, bearing the martyred Saeta in solemn procession, they left behind a scene of complete devastation.

Face drawn with sorrow, eyes red-rimmed with weeping, Padre Kino met them at Dolores, said a solemn Mass. Then the funeral procession wound slowly down the valley to Cucurpe. General Jironza led the mule which bore the box containing Saeta's remains. Padre Kino, Manje and another Jesuit walked behind. From time to time the soldiers fired their arquebuses in volleys that reverberated against the rocky walls.

As they neared the hill at Cucurpe, the padres went ahead to put on their vestments. Jironza lifted the box on his shoulders, carried it reverently to the door of the church and delivered it to the pastor. Next day as one of the padres sang the requiem Mass the church was not large enough to hold the multitude of soldiers, Indians and sorrowing Jesuits. At the end of the magnificent ceremony young Padre Saeta's body lay beneath the Epistle side of the main altar and word went out to the most remote villages concerning the veneration which was paid even to the ashes of a dead priest.

Padre Kino turned sadly back to Dolores and behind him, Chief Coxi rode along with a worried frown on his brown face. He had not understood many of the things the padres said to one another.

"The blood of a martyr is the seed of the Church." What did they mean by that? In the midst of grieving for their dead comrade they said they rejoiced, that Saeta's death would bring many souls to heaven. How could that be?

He turned to a companion riding alongside. "One thing I do know, that none of the padres seem to notice. Our Padre Kino burns with fever. Did you see how he swayed on his feet in the church? The death of his friend has pierced his heart."

Chapter 6

Vengeance!

[1695]

Chief Coxi peered through the open door of Padre Kino's little room. It was sparsely furnished. There was a table, a few books, a wooden chest, a bed—if you could call two saddle blankets on the floor a bed.

"Where is he?" asked Coxi.

The housekeeper frowned. "I do not know. Most of the time he is in the church, on his knees."

"The fever still burns him?"

"Yes. I think it gives him bad dreams. I hear him moan and cry out names—names of the dead, Saeta, Francisco. And this morning very early, before the sun was up, he talked as if to all the Pimas assembled in the church, but he was in the room alone."

"Is he there now, I wonder?" said Coxi, half to himself.

"He could be anywhere. A man with fever does strange things. I do not understand about our padre. Part of the time he is himself again. This morning, after I heard all the talking, he came out with his face very white and his eyes red. He went to the church and said Mass. When he came back he would not eat. Then he went out again. I do not know where. Why do you want him?"

"Chief Felipe is here. He has something for the padre."

"Felipe is here? He wants to see me?" It was Kino's voice. Coxi whirled to see the padre standing in the archway leading to the patio. His face was pale and drawn. A chill shook him, so that he had to hang onto the rough adobe wall. Cold sweat stood out on his face.

"I will tell the chief to come back another time," said Coxi.

"No. Bring him here." Kino walked unsteadily to a chair and sat down.

The Pima chief came through the door from a plaza brilliant with summer sun and stood blinking in the cool dimness of the room. Under his arm was a bundle and when his eyes had adjusted to the light, he came forward, knelt before Padre Kino and held it out.

"Here," he said, and Kino saw it was wrapped in a neatly tanned skin, the skin of a mountain lion, judging from its size and shape.

"What is it?" said Kino.

"It is from Tubutama," said Felipe. "Or, perhaps Caborca. I do not know."

Hands trembling, Kino unwrapped the soft leather and saw two precious vestments, one red, one white. His heart swelled with joy. Even among the rebellious Indians, there had been one who respected the vestments of a priest, had kept them from being defiled.

"Tell the people of Tubutama I thank them," he said, his voice growing stronger with each word. "Tell them too that we promise peace and a general pardon, if they will deliver up to the army the murderers of the blessed Saeta."

Chief Felipe stared at the padre. This was better than he had expected. But could he be sure? Could the soldiers be trusted?

Padre Kino said firmly, "It is true. Before we left Cucurpe, General Jironza agreed with us that this was what we should do. If the murderers are brought in, no one else will suffer. And I have a letter from the governor of Sonora. He too promises that only the guilty ones will be punished."

"When are they to be brought to the army? And where?" Felipe still wondered if it was safe to believe such generous promises.

"I will send word to you," promised Kino.

Chief Felipe hurried back across the mountain, spreading the word as he went. No Indian believed him. No one trusted the soldiers. But he repeated over and over, "Padre Kino said it was so. Padre Kino promised that everything would be as it was before, if we bring in the murderers."

But behind him, at Dolores, Padre Kino was entertaining another visitor, a wealthy Spanish gentleman from San Juan, who was the bearer of bad news. There had been trouble when General Jironza announced the plan upon which he and the Sonoran governor and the padres had agreed. The Spanish civilians at San Juan insisted that all the Indians should be punished. They were sending troops with Antonio Solis in command.

"Solis!" exclaimed Padre Kino. "Not Lieutenant Solis?"

His Spanish guest smiled. "No, not Lieutenant, Padre Kino. Antonio has been rewarded for his successful campaigns against the savages. He is now Captain Solis."

Sick with dread, Padre Kino slept little that night. But in the morning he was calm. Even the bloodthirsty Solis would not dare to break the promises of his governor and his general! The sooner this matter was settled the better. It had been a month since the murder of Padre Saeta. The murderers must be brought to justice.

Orders went from Dolores to Tubutama. "Come in peace, without weapons, to meet the army. Come to the marsh near El Tupo, between Tubutama and Magdalena."

Had the Indians, too, heard that Solis was in command? From everywhere word came back, "We are afraid to come."

Padre Kino managed to mount his horse and ride across the mountain to San Ignacio. From there he sent a message to the chief at El Tupo, telling him to summon the people. An order from Kino was not to be treated lightly. The chief took two other officials and went to Tubutama, returning with more than a hundred Indians, unarmed, carrying crosses. The innocent were bringing the guilty to justice.

Perhaps all would have been well if Padre Kino could have stayed, but the fever returned. So weak he could not stand, he clung to the saddle on the ride back to Dolores and once again, wracked with delirium, tossed from side to side on his hard bed. During lucid periods he begged for news. What was happening at the encampment beside the marsh?

For two days before the guilty Pimas were brought in, the soldiers stayed in camp, pitched near some springs in an open plain. Chief Felipe was there and on the morning of the ninth of June, Captain Solis acted as godfather at the baptism of Felipe's young son. Not long after this happy event, fifty Indians approached, put down their bows and arrows and came into the camp.

According to a prearranged plan, soldiers on horseback formed a circle around the group. Chief Felipe, along with the loyal governor from El Tupo and two other Indian officials who had been helping the Spanish, pointed out men who had taken part in the rebellion and murder. The ringleaders were not here. These Indians considered their crime so black they could not mingle with the others. They would be brought later.

Three Indians were bound. Felipe began to point out others. The Indians became fearful and began to mill around in the circle. Suddenly several of them shot between the mounted soldiers and ran for the trees. Fearful that the guilty ones would escape, Felipe seized the worst of them by the hair and said to Solis, "This is a murderer!"

With one blow of his sword, Solis cut off the man's head. The horrible sight touched off a panic and everyone in the circle made a break for freedom. The soldiers' guns were primed and ready. They aimed and fired. And when the smoke had cleared and the bloody heap of the dead was counted, forty-eight had perished, thirty of them loyal Spanish supporters.

The killing of the Tupo.

Manje took the dreadful news to Kino. The governor of El Tupo was dead. Chief Felipe was dead. "That shocked even Solis," said Manje. But afterward he admitted that Solis had given orders to kill every Indian, that if even one escaped he would cut off the head of the soldier who let him go.

Kino was prostrated with grief. This could be the end of the missions in Pima land. Could the Indians ever forget such treachery?

Manje tried to sooth him. "It may be for the best. My uncle, the general, is sure that the rebellion among the Pimas has been put down forever. Now he orders the army to Cocóspora. The soldiers go from there to the east, for a campaign against the Apaches.

Padre Kino turned his face to the wall. He knew his Pimas better than the general did.

On the morning of June 19 the troops were still at Cocóspora, awaiting word from the general. This was to be a great campaign. Perhaps they could teach the Apaches the same kind of lesson that had been taught these Pimas!

But the Pimas were far from cowed. With the soldiers out of the way, they saw their chance for revenge. Relatives of the murdered Indians and many who had, up to now, been friendly with the Spanish, joined in two large bands, went to Tubutama and Caborca and burned every building that had been spared earlier. Then three hundred of them assembled to march on Padre Campos' missions at Imuris and San Ignacio.

The padres still had friends. A heathen chief of a little village north of Imuris went down the valley and told Padre Campos what was about to happen. The general had left four soldiers at San Ignacio, so Campos felt safe in waiting there to see if the Indians actually would attack. But he sent a messenger to Cocóspora to bring back the army. The messenger was unexplainably slow and did not reach the army camp until daybreak of the 20th of June.

At eight o'clock that same morning, while Padre Campos and the four soldiers were eating breakfast at San Ignacio, they heard ear-splitting yells and the enemy was upon them. Three of the soldiers went out to fight them off while Campos put on his spurs and mounted his horse. Then the five rode off into the mountains while the yelling hordes set fire to the whole village.

While all this was happening, a second messenger had hurried on to Dolores where he warned Manje, then rode back up the mountainside to a vantage point in the pass between Dolores and San Ignacio. He did not see Campos and the soldiers make their escape and, as smoke billowed from the burning mission, mounted his horse and spurred the animal at breakneck speed for more than twenty miles back to Dolores. There he ran into the dining room, burst into tears and told between sobs that Padre Campos had been burned alive with the soldiers, the house, the church, everything!

"I must warn the general!" cried Manje and ran for his horse. It was forty miles downstream to the little town where his uncle was staying. Manje pounded into it before three in the afternoon and found General Jironza having a leisurely cup of hot chocolate. He did not finish his cup. He called for his horse; Manje got a fresh mount, and away they went up the trail, arriving as far as Cucurpe before dark. It was not safe to travel at night, so they rode up to the rectory to ask for a bed. To their relief, Padre Campos had reached there with his soldiers. It did not matter about the mission if the padre was safe!

Early next morning Manje was off for Dolores, taking two soldiers with him. Kino was alone when they arrived. That afternoon a messenger came from the west. The marauders were coming to destroy Dolores.

"We must save the sacred vessels from the altar," said Kino and that night he and Manje stole away from the village carrying boxes of ornaments, vessels, books, missals and other treasures. After stumbling through the darkness for almost two miles, the padre led the way into a cave. Far at the back of it they hid the precious things.

"This is a good place to stay," said Manje. "We should not go back to the village."

Padre Kino shook his head. "We must go back."

"Then hear my last confession." Sure that they were returning to martyrdom, Manje sank to his knees.

Padre Kino gave him absolution, and then led the way along the trail to Dolores. The sky was pink with morning when they arrived, and danger or not, Manje collapsed on his bed and went sound asleep. Padre Kino went to the church. When Manje came out after a few hours, the padre was still on his knees in front of the altar.

His prayers were answered. Not only Dolores, but the two other missions under his personal care were spared. The soldiers pursued the fleeing Indians into the mountains and killed a few of them and for a little while there was an uneasy truce. But even Padre Kino knew it could not last.

General Jironza did not have enough troops at his command to punish the rebels and sent an urgent plea for help to two Spanish generals in the east. Their campaign against the Apaches had been a success and they felt they could safely leave the border for a while. On July 13 they rode into Cocóspora to find Captain Solis there. Then General

Jironza arrived, and Padres Kino and Campos. It was the obligation of the padres to provide food for the soldiers. Many cattle and sheep that Kino had dreamed of sending to the natives of California had to go instead to feed the army.

Padre Kino was praying that there would be no more slaughter of innocent people. The Spanish generals seemed to be intelligent men, with none of Solis's bloodthirstiness. They welcomed Kino's help and advice. But they told him firmly that the rebellious Indians must be punished.

Messages went out to the villages, urging them to turn over the leaders of the revolt against the padres. They were promised pardon if they would do so, complete destruction of their homes and food supplies if they did not.

On the morning of July 20, Padre Kino said an early Mass and the army started south. Campos went along as chaplain. Five miles down the valley they halted to round up more of Kino's cattle. That afternoon Kino and Jironza left for Dolores to gather more supplies.

Deeply concerned over Kino's health, General Jironza insisted that the padre stay at Dolores. He was too weak and ill to argue, but he refused to stay in bed and spent most of the time on his knees in the church, praying for peace.

Messages came from the army. They had destroyed crops along the Altar River, seized provisions, were carrying out the grim promises they had made. They killed a few Indians at Tubutama. The rest fled into the hills. Then, as the army encamped at a ranch near Tubutama, hungry refugees began to come in. The soldiers treated them kindly and within a few days there were more than fifty Indians in the camp. The general appointed new officials for the rebellious towns from this group. He must have had a great deal of confidence in them, for he wrote to Padre Kino:

"Peace is as good as made. I will give my head for any misdeed the Pimas commit after this!"

In two areas, however, the Indians were still suspicious and fearful. At Caborca, where another general had taken his troops, the people remained in hiding. So did the ones who lived near the place where Solis had killed so many. Nothing the army could do would induce them to show themselves. The generals appealed to Kino to come and help them.

Still thin and weak, Padre Kino arrived on August 21. He had sent the Indian governor of Dolores ahead with messages to several ranches. Some of the newly appointed Indian governors came to meet him and gradually other Pimas drifted in, until he had assembled a sizeable delegation. There was a formal conference. The Indians agreed to meet at Tubutama, to bring with them those who were in hiding. But there was still no message from the Pimas of Caborca and Kino decided he would go there himself.

"I will send soldiers with you," said the general, but Kino shook his head.

"I have offered to go in peace," he said. "Soldiers will only make the Indians distrust me."

With only one sergeant and a number of friendly Indians, Padre Kino went toward Caborca. The general encamped there with eighty soldiers was quite willing to let Kino take charge.

"Have you any captives?" asked the padre.

"Two women and three little girls," said the general.

"Release one of the women," ordered Kino. "Send her to summon her people. Tell them the Boat Man is here."

The name was magic. Day by day more Indians came to see the padre. He talked with each of them, renewed old friendships, questioned them about Padre Saeta's death. They confirmed what he had been told by Chief Felipe. The people of Caborca had not killed Saeta. It was wicked Indians from Tubutama who did it.

So Kino and the soldiers returned to Tubutama. On August 30, a great peace conference was held. Padre Kino said Mass at the nearest mission and Padre Campos at the military camp. The Indians made speeches. They were sorry for the death of Padre Saeta and the good Indians killed with him. They were sorry for the burning of the missions. They grieved for the eighty Pimas who had been slaughtered by the soldiers. They pledged themselves to seek out and deliver, alive or dead, the murderers of Padre Saeta.

Through it all Padre Kino and the generals listened gravely. At the end the Indians begged that the missions be restored, the padres come back to them.

"We will receive the padres with love," they promised. "And we will rebuild everything that has been destroyed."

Kino rose from his place and threw his arms around the speaker. The generals followed his example and Pima governors and captains gathered round to share in the embraces.

Would it be a lasting peace? Padre Kino believed it would. He was even more hopeful after his return to Dolores when he received the news contained in a letter from Lieutenant Manje.

"Captain Solis has been discharged by the army," wrote the lieutenant. "He has gone to the capital of Mexico, publicly disgraced."

Padre Kino breathed his thanks to heaven. Now, if he had to summon the Flying Column, it would not be Solis who commanded it! And now, he hoped, after so many bitter lessons, the Spanish leaders would treat his Indians with fairness.

Chapter 7

THE CHILDREN ASKED FOR BREAD

[1695]

Once again the skies were blue above Dolores. Free from threats of fire and death, in the heat of a September afternoon everyone slumbered, or nodded over his work. Everyone, that is, except Padre Kino.

"What is he doing?" whispered Marcos, son of the new captain general of Dolores, squatting on his heels in the shade of the patio wall.

The fat cook yawned. "He writes a book."

Marcos stared at her. Books he knew. There was the big book in the church. When he served the Mass he carried it from one side of the altar to the other. And there was a small black book that the padre carried with him and read every day, even on their longest journeys. There were books on the table in the padre's room. But write a book? How could you do that? He looked at the cook, drowsing over the big basket of cucumbers she had brought in from the garden. No use asking her anything. He would go to his father.

The captain general nodded wisely at the question. Yes, Padre Kino was writing a book. It was like writing a message, except it took longer. "You have waited while the padre wrote to someone," said the official. "You saw how he used the pen."

The boy grinned. "*Sí, Señor*—and got a box on the ears for asking too many questions."

"The padre is angry only when you show disrespect for holy things," reproved his father. "And you must not bother him now, because he writes all about the young Saeta and how he died. And there will be much about Dolores, too, and the other missions, and about all of us. The padre told me."

"Well," said Marcos, "I wish he would hurry. As soon as he has finished writing, he is going to take me to the capital. That is what the padre told *me*." Marcos had no idea what the capital was, nor of the fifteen hundred miles that lay between it and Dolores. Throughout September, October and half of November his impatience grew, but still Padre Kino spent long hours in his room, his pen scratching, scratching. The book was for the provincial, the viceroy. Perhaps it would go to Rome. He must not forget anything.

In 1694, when Kino had returned from the trip with Manje, during which they had gazed across at California from the mountain peak west of Caborca, the padre had asked that he be allowed to come to Mexico City for a conference with the provincial. The permission was granted, but when news got around that he was leaving, a torrent of protests poured in to the provincial from soldiers, officials, private citizens and missionaries in the land of the Pimas. Kino could not be spared. He must stay where he was.

Now there was peace, however, and the Pimas, as grateful for the treaty as Kino himself, had begun to restore the mission properties. Fortunately, adobe did not burn, so when

Kino writes his work, Heavenly Favors.

the debris was cleared away, all they had to build were new roofs. They had been promised that the padres would come to them once again as soon as the villages were ready for them. And the lean months which followed the destruction of the crops along the Altar River made life under the protection of the padres seem more attractive than ever.

The murderers of Padre Saeta were still unpunished, but they could be taken care of later. They would cause no more trouble. It was quite safe for Padre Kino to leave his charges for a while. And he had even more reasons than before to go to the capital. The ex-captain Solis, trying to excuse himself for his brutalities against the Pimas, had told many lies about them and made personal accusations against Kino himself. There was only one way to deal with such accusations and that was in person.

As soon as the book was finished, Kino put Padre Campos in charge at Dolores and headed south. Right behind him rode Marcos and in the pack train were several other Pima boys, the best-looking, most intelligent ones at Dolores. Padre Kino was not only going to brag about his Indians, he was going to show some of them to the skeptics.

The train proceeded at a steady "Kino-pace" which covered about thirty miles a day. Each morning the padre said Mass. On Christmas Day they were in Guadalajara, only four hundred miles from Mexico City. The wide-eyed Marcos watched with the others while Kino said the three masses of the Feast of the Nativity in a new church named for Our Lady of Loreto. Then they were off again, to arrive in the capital on January 8, 1696.

Marcos recognized the hawk-nosed man who greeted them. It was Padre Salvatierra, who had come to Dolores on Christmas Eve, six years before, and traveled with Padre Kino into Arizona. Marcos had been a very small boy then, but no one could forget the kindly Salvatierra. He and Kino appeared together often in the capital and Marcos, trotting behind them, heard over and over again the word *California*, as the two padres urged the provincial and the viceroy to re-establish the missions there.

Kino had other requests. His memory was long. At the court of the viceroy he told the story of the wicked soldier who destroyed an Indian town when Kino first went to Dolores. The soldier escaped punishment, said Kino, and the Indians were not permitted to return to their lands. He realized that nothing could be done about the soldier who had apparently left the country, but pleaded that the Indians be given their town again, and beamed in happy gratitude when the viceroy granted his plea.

The petition for California was not so successful. Although everyone agreed that the missions should be reopened, money was still not available for the venture.

When it came to the lies told by Solis about the Pimas, Padre Kino said flatly that such arrogant officers as Solis were responsible for the recent Indian uprisings!

"Look at these Pima boys!" cried Kino, indicating Marcos and his neatly dressed, quiet and polite companions. "The children of Tubutama and Caborca are no different from them. And there are thousands like them in Pima land."

There were tears in Kino's eyes as he pleaded for the children. No one would ever forget him standing there in his shabby black robe, stocky figure shrunken by the months of fever, but feet firmly planted, head thrown back, his eloquence carrying them from the brilliant Spanish court to the humble villages from which these children came.

Even more eloquent than Kino's speeches was the book which he presented to the provincial. The first part of it, about Saeta's murder and the events which followed, was about what the provincial had already been told, for the news had spread through Mexico with incredible speed. But the rest of the book, and the greater part of it, was about the riches of Pima land. The provincial read with growing amazement, for it sounded like Paradise, and the Pimas almost like angels!

Kino had listed the missions one by one—Dolores, San Ignacio and Imuris, Magdalena, Caborca and, last of all, Cocóspora, high on a hill above the river, about thirty miles north of Dolores. Untouched by the rebellion, the mission had extensive lands with forests, fertile fields and orchards, a house and a little church. Most important of all, Cocóspora was on the road to the north in Arizona, where hundreds of natives in large towns were begging for missionaries to come and live among them. They had built houses for the padres, were growing fields of wheat and corn for the Church. The Father Visitor and other padres, and a number of civil authorities had promised them priests, but no priests had gone to them.

Then, Kino's book came back to his martyred friend, Padre Saeta, blaming his death on the resentment which the Indians felt because they needed the fathers, and the fathers did not come.

"The children asked for bread," wrote Padre Kino, "and there was no one to break it unto them."

It was a powerful argument and it was accompanied by a large and detailed historical map of Jesuit New Spain. There were few map makers in the New World. This map alone would cause a sensation.

The provincial made his decision. Five new missionaries would go to the Pimas. Padre Kino could scarcely wait to get home with the news. On February 8, he headed north. He stopped at one of the missions for Holy Week. Where the road turned east, toward Bazerac, Kino turned into it. He must go there to see Padre Polici, who had been appointed Father Visitor of the region for the next three years.

But he sent the rest of his party on to the Dolores with messages to the Pima chiefs. He wanted to see them. June would be a good time. And he bid them all to come. He had good news for them.

The trip to Bazerac took more time than he had counted on. There were several conferences with Polici. And when he wanted to ride on, the Apache sympathizers in that region were on a rampage and Kino had to wait for an army escort. One might wonder who was taking care of whom, because when he left his escort briefly to visit two Jesuit friends, the captain of the troop, his son, and all his men were killed by the Indians. Padre Kino went on safely, and alone.

It was mid-May when he reached Dolores. Padre Campos had not been happy there. He had almost decided to ask for a transfer, to leave Pima country forever, but Kino was so enthusiastic about plans for the future, Campos finally agreed to go back to San Ignacio.

By mid-June the wheat was golden, ready for the harvest, and the chiefs Kino had summoned assembled at Dolores. Padre Kino spoke to them in their own language. He told them how glad he was to be home again.

He gave them greetings from the viceroy, the new provincial, the new Father Visitor. They listened gravely, with appreciation. Such greetings befitted their dignity as chiefs. They thanked the padre for bringing them. After the meeting some of the visiting Indians were questioned and those who had had sufficient instruction in the Faith were baptized. Others were told they must wait. They must learn more about God.

Then everybody pitched in to help with the wheat. They cut it with hand sickles and some of them were very skillful. For that matter, most of them had helped Padre Kino with other harvests. It was an honor to help their padre. And besides, when they helped him they helped themselves as well. Every grain of that wheat would go to feed the Pimas, or be traded at the Spanish settlements for clothing to keep the Pimas warm.

When they had gone to their own villages, Kino made a formal report of the assembly, listed the Indians who had taken part, and sent it to the capital of Mexico. If the provincial needed any further evidence of Pima loyalty, this should furnish it. These were the children who asked for bread. Let more priests come speedily to give it to them!

The blessing of food.

Chapter 8

AN ERROR IN THE MAP

[1698]

During the two years following Padre Kino's trip to Mexico City he established missions to the north, in Arizona, stocked them with cattle, sheep, and goats, made frequent trips to instruct the people in the Holy Faith.

One day in midsummer of the year 1698 he was at Remedios. The church was not yet finished, but the walls were more than nine feet high and branches had been intertwined to make a leafy roof. Padre Kino looked out at the sea of dark heads, many from the distant missions he had established, bowed in reverence at the end of a solemn Mass. There were a few Spanish gentlemen from a nearby mining town, but most of the crowd were Pimas, come here to kneel before the altar, to worship God and pay honor to Our Lady. All had marched in the procession that morning, carrying a beautiful new statue of Our Lady of Remedios through the village named for her, installing it here beside the altar. How sad it was that such faithful people must go back to missions without padres and which he himself could visit so rarely.

In the throng he recognized Chief Coro, and Chief Humari from the San Pedro River, and the Pima captain and governor from Bac. There was another Indian governor from a village on the Gila River two hundred and fifty miles away. What wonderful people they were!

Padre Kino began to speak. This, he said, had been a year of great tragedy, but of triumphs even greater. The Apaches had driven the padre from the mission at Cocóspora and destroyed the church, the house, the whole village. Another small settlement near Chief Coro's town of Quiburi had been sacked and some of its people killed. But the valiant Coro had gathered five hundred Pimas and avenged the murders, fighting hand to hand with the Apache chief, and, when he had killed him, pursuing the Apaches and killing or wounding more than three hundred of them. When the news of that great victory reached San Juan, General Jironza himself summoned Chief Coro to the fort, so that he might be suitably rewarded.

"There is peace throughout the lands of the Pimas," Kino ended. "At many of your towns are ranches where you are raising sheep and cattle, and fields for the growing of all kinds of grain. Tend them well, so that the padres for whom you ask may come to you."

Kino dismissed them and they turned to the feast that had been prepared, hunger whetted by the smell of roasting beef which had drifted from the cooking fires since daybreak. Some of the more important chiefs were given hot chocolate to drink. When they left Remedios they were a happy lot, well fed, and excited over the prospect of seeing Padre Kino again soon.

"Within eight or ten days I must go to the Gila River and

the Sea of California," he had said. "Tell the new people of the coast that I am coming." The chiefs hurried homeward, each of them hoping he would be chosen to go with the padre as guide and companion.

Padre Kino hurried home too. He was feeling feverish and weak again. He would have to rest a little before this next journey, but while he rested, he could plan. He *must* find an overland route to California if it existed! The reasons were more pressing than ever.

Padre Salvatierra had been in California since the previous September, and had taken up exactly where Padre Kino left off twelve years before. His letters made Padre Kino weep, but they were tears of joy, for the Indians of Lower California had forgotten neither Kino nor the Faith. Hulo had turned up with his father, and while poor Chief Ibo was dying of cancer, Kino's prayers for him had been answered, for Salvatierra had arrived in time to baptize him. The lists of Indian and Spanish words compiled by Kino and the other padres were a great help, and it seemed that at last a permanent mission had been established on the inhospitable shores of California.

But the same difficulties suffered by Kino and Admiral Atondo were recurring. The Sea of California was as rough and treacherous as ever and although there were more plentiful supplies on the mainland than there had been during the drought of 1685, it cost more to ship them. "I paid six thousand dollars to ship twenty cattle from Mexico to California!" wrote Salvatierra and Padre Kino nodded unhappily as he read.

He put down the letter and closed his eyes. The fever made him a little lightheaded. He knew very well he was here in Dolores, on his own hard bed, yet all at once it seemed he was at Jesuit headquarters, in Mexico City, saying to the provincial, "I will explore the country far to the north and west, find out for myself whether California is island or peninsula!"

How long ago was it when he made those brave plans? Twelve years. He had been at Dolores for twelve years and he still had not traced the mysterious Sea of California to its northern boundaries.

A chill shook him, but he fought it off, pulled the blanket tightly around his shoulders and made himself sit up. When his head cleared he struggled to his feet, got to the door and called for young Marcos. The fat housekeeper bustled, scolding, from the kitchen, but at Kino's insistence, called the young Pima foreman. When Marcos appeared, Padre Kino fired a whole string of orders.

"What are you saying?" cried Marcos, not waiting for the padre to finish. "North, west—where are we going? Who is going with us? You are too sick to travel anywhere, I think."

To Marcos's amazement, color was coming back into Padre Kino's face. He dropped the blanket to the floor, straightened, walked with almost his customary firm step to the door opening onto the plaza and threw it wide.

"Hand me that stick," he commanded. "I will show you where we are going," and he began to draw a map on the dusty earth. "We go north, through Bac to the Gila River. That river runs west, is it not so? We follow, to the west. When we reach the Sea, we turn south toward Caborca. It is a long journey and by the time we reach there, our pack animals will be tired, so we will exchange them for fresh ones. Do you see? No? Well, do what I tell you, anyway. We will leave in the morning. General Jironza is sending a Captain Carrasco to go with me."

Marcos hurried away, shaking his head. He had heard all

about the proposed journey, knew, in fact, that the military escort was due in Dolores today, but neither he nor anyone else in the village had believed Padre Kino could possibly recover in time to leave tomorrow. Something must have happened to cure him, thought Marcos. A miracle. That was it. Surely the great St. Francis Xavier must have done it!

Two days later the pack train crossed the divide at about the spot where Nogales, Arizona, would one day stand, and headed down the fertile valley of the Santa Cruz River. They were met at Bac by Chief Coro, and the Spanish officer, Carrasco, listened to this Indian military leader with admiration and approval.

"I have moved my people from Quiburi for a while," said Coro. "The Apaches are thirsty for our blood. We will stay away from the border until they forget a little."

Captain Carrasco nodded. "It is a wise general who knows when to retreat a little."

He strolled away to look over the town and Coro said, "Where are the rest of the soldiers? Was the captain not afraid to come alone?"

Padre Kino smiled. "If he was afraid at first, he is so no longer. We have been welcomed everywhere, as always."

"And where do you go now?" asked Coro, hoping he would be invited to go along. He was disappointed when Kino outlined the journey and mentioned the guides waiting for him at the river.

The padre was not as well as he looked. Two days later he was forced to give up climbing a mountain from the top of which he hoped to trace the course of the river. But after a day's rest he insisted they go on. The guides had given him disturbing information. Instead of running west, they said, the Gila River turned south in a big bend. There were many villages to the south. They all wanted Padre Kino to visit them.

"If the river truly does run south," said Kino, "we can go in that direction and reach the place where it empties into the Sea of California."

Captain Carrasco had his doubts about the river being anywhere near when the party started south the morning of October 2. It looked like desert country to him. And their only water supply was what could be carried in gourds. At noon the padre permitted each man a sip of water, just one sip, and as the afternoon sun crossed a cloudless sky, the captain began to calculate how far they had come and whether they had enough water to take them safely to the next spring— if there were springs in this desert.

They had traveled about thirty miles when a cry came from the head of the column. "Someone comes!"

Carrasco strained his eyes to see, blinked against the glare of late afternoon and looked again. Four Indians approached. On the shoulder of each was a tall pottery jar and as the party rode up they welcomed it with plentiful draughts of the most delicious cool water Captain Carrasco had ever tasted.

Soon he glimpsed a field of melons, green and welcoming among their drying vines. Then they were in a little village with more than sixty Indians lined up with gifts of corn, beans and watermelons. No white man had ever visited them, but they had heard of Padre Kino.

The next night they were welcomed by over seven hundred Indians with flaring torches, found a house prepared for them, crosses erected along the road, arches across it. Fires burned in front of the houses and the warmth felt good to Carrasco. The days were still hot at this time of year, but as the sun dropped, so did the temperature. By midnight he was chilled in spite of the fire and glad to roll in his blankets inside the little adobe house. Padre Kino did not seem to notice. He was still talking to the chiefs and headmen when Carrasco dropped off to sleep. And he shook the captain awake next morning just as the sun's first rays slanted across the village roofs. Time for Mass.

Was there no limit to the good padre's endurance? wondered Carrasco. He himself was too tired to get up; besides he was worried. The Pimas of the party had been carrying on a running argument among themselves for three days concerning the route they followed.

"So far there has been water, yet who knows when there will be only sand?" said a muleteer.

Padre Kino heard him and met the objection head on. "We will load one of your mules with gourds and water jars. Get some crates built to hold them, so they will be ready."

"But, Padre," said a second, "even if we have water, there is no grass near the coast."

"Then we will carry grass with us," said Kino.

"It is not water and grass that concerns me," grumbled a man from Dolores. "Even at this time of year, the heat at the Sea of California burns so you cannot stand it."

"Mules will not travel if it gets that hot," said the driver of the train.

"Then we will travel at night." Padre Kino turned to the chief of the village. "Bring the old woman here—the one who came today from the coast with snails and little shells from the Sea."

The old woman, stooped from carrying a pack, approached the group. "Look at her," said Kino. "She came alone from the very shores of the Sea. How can men like you refuse to make the journey?"

One by one they shrugged and turned away. Carrasco noticed that thereafter they traveled with more confidence. Even the mules seemed to walk a little faster. The following day they reached the little village of Sonoita and here the map maker acquired some new guides and a great deal of encouragement regarding the rest of his proposed journey.

"You will not need to carry water with you," said the chief. "The Sea is near and there is water and grass on the way."

And so it was. A ride of forty miles around the south end of a mountain was blessed with a good road, plenty of water, grass and the waving leaves of spiky reeds which always meant a swampy area. That night while they were eating calabashes prepared for them by friendly natives, Kino questioned the guides.

"How far to the Sea?"

"It is very near." The native pointed. "From the top of the mountain you can see the mouth of the Gila River."

"Yes," nodded the chief, "and beyond it, on the very big Colorado River, there are people who have big fields of corn and beans and cotton. Calabashes, too."

Kino's eyes shone. He turned to Carrasco. "Let us go to see those people."

But Carrasco had had enough. "We have no relay animals," he said, "and who knows how far these can travel?"

Reluctantly, Kino agreed. "But if I cannot go to the mouth of the Gila, or the river beyond, I will see it from this mountain," he vowed, and next day rode with the guides seventeen miles up a rough trail to the summit. During the long climb he wondered, and prayed. Would this be the day he found the answer to his question? Would he be able to see California, across the wide waters? And the Sea of California, suppose he saw its northern limits! He prayed he might—

but when he reached the summit, the air was hazy. Below them stretched the Sea, and that was clear enough, with sand dunes between it and the mountain. But beyond? His eyes could not pierce the haze.

"What do you see to the north?" Kino asked the guide.

"I do not see very much," said the Indian, "but I know what is there. Far up that way the Gila River and the Colorado River come together. Then they flow southward into the Sea."

"Are you sure?" cried Kino. Much as he wanted to believe the fellow he could not. He would have to go and see for himself. It meant another journey, an even longer one—but he had learned enough to know that he must make changes in his latest map. On it he had drawn the Gila and the Colorado flowing side by side, each emptying into the Sea at a different place. If they flowed together—but he still did not know whether California was island or peninsula.

On the tedious hundred-and-thirty-mile ride south to Caborca, Padre Kino was silent much of the time, his mind busy with a new map, with plans for an expedition from Dolores to Sonoita and northwest to the place where the Gila joined the Colorado.

At Caborca they picked up fresh pack animals, but before they headed east toward Dolores, Padre Kino took Carrasco out to look at the boat, begun four years ago when Lieutenant Manje helped to fell the cottonwood tree. Captain Carrasco had heard the story and looked with interest at the shaped timbers and keel. They looked very odd out here in the desert, but there was one good thing about a dry climate: wood did not deteriorate. Now that Padre Kino had once again received permission to work on the boat—for there had been another change in the Father Visitors and the new one would like to see the boat completed—Kino gave orders to some of the men to cut boards for the deck.

Captain Carrasco shook his head, stopped, looked at Kino and marveled. If Padre Kino said so, the boat would probably be finished and taken to the Sea. It might even float! This Kino could do anything. Just ask a man who had traveled with him for a month!

They went on to Dolores where Carrasco said good-bye to Padre Kino and hurried on to San Juan. There the captain made a long report to General Jironza. They had traveled almost eight hundred miles in twenty-five days. Kino had baptized four hundred Indians and Carrasco had counted more than four thousand people, handed out more than forty canes of office.

"Padre Kino must be well satisfied with his expedition," said the general, but Carrasco shook his head.

"I do not think so. All he can talk about is an error on his map and his next journey to the northwest."

Chapter 9

THE DEVIL'S HIGHWAY

[1699]

It had not looked far to Padre Kino from the top of the mountain near Sonoita to the place where the Indians said the Gila River flowed into the Colorado. But distances are deceptive in the clear, dry, desert air. What appeared to be fifty miles was well over a hundred and twenty. And the terrain was some of the most difficult in all Sonora and Arizona for the traveler, so difficult it became known as El Camino del Diablo, the Devil's Highway.

It held no fears for Kino, but as an experienced traveler he made more elaborate preparations for this expedition than for the earlier one. On the 16th of February, 1699, when he arrived once more in Sonoita, his equipment included eight loads of provisions and eighty horses. In addition he had his Pimas drive thirty-six cattle from Dolores, with which he intended to establish a ranch. For Padre Kino meant to make this little village of Sonoita a base headquarters for further explorations in the northwest.

The Kino livestock.

With Kino was his old friend Manje, a captain now, acting as military escort. They followed their customary procedure at Sonoita, with Manje talking through an interpreter to the chiefs and the padre preaching to the people. All day and all night he preached and the sleepy Manje had a hard time to keep awake during the early morning Mass.

They left their tired horses at Sonoita and were riding fresh ones, but even these did not have much stamina. On the second day of travel, crossing barren plains with no pasture, the horses began to weaken. After a three-day ride through treeless mountains, finding only water here and there in natural tanks in the deep rock and almost no food for their sullen animals, they reached a place which, the guides said, was not far from the Gila River. But that night their horses could go no farther, and as there was a little water here, they struck camp.

It seemed like a miracle to find trees and grass the next morning. It was too early in the year for the most nourishing forage, but by that time the starving animals would have eaten the bark from the trees. They grazed all day along the banks of the river, filling their paunches with the spring grass.

As usual, Manje was counting Indians and observing their peculiarities. These were a mixed tribe, Pimas and Yumas. The men wore no clothes at all, the women nothing above the waist. They were a handsome lot and much lighter in color than the Indians of Sonora.

The next day a hundred Yuma men came from a settlement eight miles farther down the river. The padre preached to them, and Manje presented a few small gifts along with a beribboned cane. They brought gifts of their own to these strange white men—gourds full of flour and beans and bread made from the fruit of a tree. Having established the fact that they were friends through the exchange of gifts, Padre Kino began to question the newcomers about the distance to the Sea and the place where the rivers emptied into it.

"One says it is a journey of six days," reported the interpreter, "but another says it is only three."

"We cannot take you to see it," said the Yumas. "We fear the people who live there."

"I am going anyway," said Captain Manje stubbornly. "I have not come all this distance to turn back now.

Padre Kino put a hand on his arm. "These Indians do not know us. For the present we must do as they say."

"We cannot even go to see where this river empties into the Colorado?"

"No, my son," said Kino, "we cannot."

Manje looked at him. The good padre was as exhausted as his horses had been. His face was drawn, his eyes heavy.

"Go and rest," said Manje abruptly. "I will ride to the top of that high mountain to the west. The interpreter will go with me." And he set out as soon as his horses could be caught and saddled.

"I saw the place where the rivers join," he reported that evening, "but it was too foggy to see anything else."

"I am glad to know about the rivers," said Padre Kino, then, his eyes brightening, "I have been making discoveries, too. Some of the old Indians here remember a white man who came many years ago with horses and soldiers."

"That must have been Onate, one of our explorers," said Manje. "He came through this country almost a hundred years ago. I doubt if anyone here remembers him."

"Perhaps their fathers told them," Kino smiled. "But they themselves saw a wondrous thing when they were boys. A beautiful white woman, dressed in white, gray and blue, in a dress that came clear to her feet, appeared to them and spoke of God. Some of the Indians shot her with arrows, but they could not kill her. She went away, but in a few days she came back."

"Padre," exclaimed Manje, "I heard the same story at Sonoita. I did not believe it—but if these Indians saw her too—"

Kino nodded. Young Manje and he were thinking of the miraculous appearances in this new world of a Spanish nun, Maria de Agreda who, although she never left her convent in Spain, preached again and again to the Indians of New Mexico. So, she had come here, too.

"That was about seventy years ago," mused Kino. "These old chiefs are at least eighty. They could remember her. It is possible."

His blue eyes looked westward. "They tell of other travelers.

North and west of here is the ocean. White men sometimes come from there to trade. No one knows who they are, but they come overland from the ocean. Do you know what that means?"

Manje laughed. "How do you know they come overland? You must not believe everything these Indians tell you, Padre Kino! If men came from the ocean, on land all the way, it would mean that California is a peninsula, when we know it has to be an island or Sir Francis Drake could not have sailed around it!"

Kino frowned but held his tongue. He was not ready for an argument on this question. Not yet. He picked up a big blue shell and Manje, glad to change the subject said, "What have you there?"

Kino handed it over and Manje said, "Why it is like the shell you keep on the table, at Dolores." Kino nodded. The natives had brought him several of the big abalone shells this morning, the first he had seen since that long-ago trip to the west coast of California. Where had these come from? he wondered. Had traders brought them from the shores of the Pacific Ocean? Impossible to find the answer on this expedition, but perhaps the next time he came, he could make friends with the Indians farther down the river. Perhaps they would know.

The next morning they started east along the south bank of the Gila River. Again they traversed strange country, but it was a pleasant journey, always within sight of cottonwood trees, with plenty of water and pasture for the horses. In six days they were back in familiar territory. On March 7 they were at San Xavier del Bac, where thirteen hundred people assembled to celebrate their arrival.

It rained that day, a heavy downpour that sent the river

out of its banks and made seas of mud out of the roads. Padre Kino was happy to stay awhile and proud to show what the people of Bac could do. They had harvested and stored a hundred bushels of wheat in an adobe house. The cattle and horses had increased many times since Padre Kino brought the stock to them.

Two days later it was still raining, but Padre Kino insisted on leaving. Before they had gone five miles, a violent hurricane began to blow. The horses stopped in their tracks. It was impossible to go on. They spent a miserable night in the open and Padre Kino's fever returned. His feet and legs were swollen with rheumatism and Manje wished with all his heart that they were back with the friendly natives of Bac.

In the morning Padre Kino insisted that they go on. After a few miles, however, one of the servants shouted and Manje saw the padre leaning over his saddle horn, almost unconscious. By the time they got him off his horse, he had fainted. Hastily the Indians made camp and all that day Kino tossed on his blankets, nauseated, fevered, his poor legs swollen so he could not find comfort in any position.

The next day he managed to swallow some medicine and keep it down; the pains left him and the swelling decreased. He was able to mount his horse and continue the journey. The river was too high to cross and they continued along the west bank until they came to a large village. The Indians brought over a sheep, butchered it and made some broth.

"He is so sick, so weak!" said one of them, looking sorrowfully down at Kino.

Manje frowned. Padre Kino was too ill to travel, but he could not stay out in the open. They pressed on, arriving at Dolores on the 14th of March. As they went into the church to thank God for bringing them safely back, no one was more grateful than Captain Manje. Yet no one looked forward with more eagerness than he to a second northwest expedition. Like Kino, he remembered only the good.

While Captain Manje was making his official report, Padre Kino was writing long letters to everyone he knew. At some time during that desperate ride from the Gila River, he had become convinced that in spite of Manje's objections, his own long-ago idea concerning California was the true one. It was not an island. It was a peninsula!

He took the big blue abalone shells from the packs and compared them to the one he had brought from the west coast of California. Bigger than a man's hand, heavy, with a dark blue coating on the outside, and inside iridescent shades of brilliant blue and green winking up at him. They were the same. There was no doubt of it. These new ones must have been brought from the Pacific Coast by the strange white men the Yumas and Pimas had described to him.

California *was* a peninsula, he *could* supply Salvatierra and his missions by driving stock around the head of the Sea. He must write Salvatierra at once! And he must tell the men of Caborca to stop work on the boat. It was no longer needed.

But before that letter was written, a messenger arrived with an amazing communication from Salvatierra. He had not heard from Kino for months, but the two of them had reached the same conclusion at almost the same time.

"We are desirous of knowing," wrote Salvatierra, "whether from that new coast which Your Reverence traversed, California may be seen and what sign there is on that side whether this narrow sea is landlocked."

Chapter 10

Visit from Salvatierra

[1701]

A year and a half after Kino's momentous journey with Manje, Padre Salvatierra was finally able to leave California to see his old friend in the Pima country. On February 21, 1701, he rode up the river to Dolores and an enthusiastic welcome from Padre Kino. Captain Manje was there too, but he missed the best of the reunion that night when the two old friends talked until almost morning. The Apaches again! Manje and most of his soldiers were called away in the late afternoon to aid a hard-pressed Spanish town.

"Are you sure you are right about the peninsula?" Salvatierra's dark, weather-beaten face, with its great beak of a nose, thrust forward eagerly as he asked the question.

"I am sure," said Kino flatly. "In October I went once again to the Gila River—"

The yellow candle flame flickered in the cold draft from the shuttered window. Neither man noted the chill. Kino was once again on the hilltop with the Indians who had gone with him from Dolores, gazing south, west and southwest over thirty leagues (seventy-five miles) of level country, without any sea, looking down upon the junction of the Colorado River with the Gila and their many groves and fields.

"There was no sea?" repeated Salvatierra.

Kino shook his head. "We were above the head of the Gulf."

"Then what did you do? Go on to the south?"

"No. The Pima guides were tired. Besides, the time had come to collect cattle for the missions of California."

Salvatierra nodded. He was grateful for the generosity of the missions of Sonora, but he had hoped for more proof than this that the Sea of California did not go on and on for hundreds of miles to the north.

"So, you turned back?" he asked.

"We were just starting east when a chief of the Yumas appeared," said Padre Kino. "We had given him the cane of office the year before and now he begged with tears in his eyes that I go to see his people. The pack train had already set out, but I stayed to talk to this chief and at last I decided it was a matter of conscience to go to see the Yumas."

He smiled. "I was glad for the decision the next morning, after Mass, when I went down the river with the chief and met more than forty of his people who had traveled all night, fearing I would leave without seeing them."

He went on to describe the town at the junction of the two rivers, where he was welcomed by more than a thousand people. Two hundred others came that afternoon and the next day three hundred more. He talked to them throughout the day and far into the night.

"Then," he said, "I started back up the Gila River and once again I turned aside to climb another peak, a higher one this time. From the top I saw a large stretch of country in California. The two rivers, below the place where they joined, ran united about twenty-five miles to the west, turned south, and about fifty miles farther on, emptied into the head of the Sea of California."

Padre Salvatierra straightened with a great sigh that almost blew out the flickering candle. California was not an island! Let others say what they would. He was convinced.

The next morning he set out for Caborca, stopping on the way to visit two other missions, while Padre Kino made a hurried trip to check on the fortifications at Cocóspora. The two met again at Caborca on March 9 and Manje joined them there the same day. The pack train left for Sonoita in the afternoon, the rest of the caravan next morning.

Most of the road to Sonoita was easy enough, but the route they chose thereafter was marked by more hardships than were recorded on any of Kino's other journeys. When they finally reached the Sea of California, Salvatierra felt that it was all worthwhile, however, for across the water he could see California, with its spiny range of mountains distant no more than twenty to thirty miles.

In the north the mountains on both sides of the Sea curved toward each other, but to the disappointment of the padres, they could not get an unobstructed view of the whole. And the springs they had found in these billows of sand were so low after one day's watering that only thirty animals could drink. There was no hope of going on to the north as they had planned. They must turn back.

Before they reached Sonoita they turned aside to climb another high peak, this one so steep they had to go up on all fours. As they reached the top the sun was setting and in the clear light they saw the Sea spread out below them, the

Kino and Salvatierra on Cerro del Pinacate observe the California Peninsula.

horrible sand dunes through which they had been struggling, the beach where they had picked up all manner of shells except the big blue ones.

Another thing was plain, to Salvatierra and Kino, at least. The California mountains ran northward, curved a bit and joined the mountains of New Spain on the mainland.

"I was far beyond the head of the Sea last October," said Kino.

Captain Manje's lip curled. He had not been with Kino on that last trip and he doubted, frankly, that the good padre had been where he thought he had. Manje could not see that the two mountain ranges came together. He did not argue with the others, but he set his stubborn jaw and stuck to his original opinion. Let the two padres say what they liked, Captain Manje knew that California was an island! And that was not the only subject he disagreed on with Padre Kino. One day soon he would speak his mind about the way Kino pampered the Indians.

So this time as they turned homeward to Dolores, it was Manje who rode in silence while Kino and Salvatierra chattered of the land route to California as if they had already traversed it. That was the way they wrote of it, too, when they made a report of their journey. And Kino titled his new map, "Land Passage to California and its Neighboring New Nations and New Missions of the Company of Jesus in North America."

The following April, a year later, in 1702, Kino summed up his findings. He had made two more trips to the Gila and Colorado in that time. Twice he had seen the head of the Gulf. Traveling down the Colorado River from its junction with the Gila to its mouth, no Sea of California had been found or seen. At the mouth of the Colorado River, Kino had seen the sun rise over the head of the Gulf. Natives there brought him blue shells from the other ocean, ten days distant. And Indians from the southwest told of the Jesuits in California and described their vestments.

"Finally," wrote Kino, "if some hostile and obstinate persons should maintain that some Indians say that further west the sea extends to the northwest, those Indians speak of the other sea, the Pacific Ocean, and not of our Sea of California."

Then, almost as if he knew Manje's doubts and hoped to shake them out of him, Padre Kino asked the captain for a certificate that what Kino had written was true. It would have been better not to ask.

"The report and the signature are Kino's," wrote Manje evasively. "Kino has brought about the conversion of the Pima nation and founded many ranches. The Gulf west of Santa Clara Mountain is only thirty miles wide. As to the rest, I have not witnessed all, but I do assert confidently that the report is by a zealous minister to whom I give entire credit."

What had he said? Nothing. Padre Kino might have persisted, taken Manje on another expedition, convinced him that the padres were right. But Manje was becoming a man of business, of property. He did not see much of Kino any more. And Kino was like a father who has so many children he cannot worry about one for more than a few moments until some of the others demand his attention.

The Apaches to the north and west of the Gila River had replied with friendly messages to a plea sent them through a chief from the Pima border. At peace with their Pima neighbors, it looked for a while as if Kino might be able to establish a mission among the hostile tribes. Apache outbreaks in another part of the country made everyone cautious, however, and Kino was told to build up his own missions and forget about expansion for a time.

Death had depleted the ranks of the padres. In one summer they lost Kino's old friend, Padre Gonzalez, who became ill on one of the Colorado River expeditions with Kino, was brought home in a litter, carried by faithful Pimas, and died at Tubutama. Within a month the padre who buried him was dead. And in the heat of midsummer, the padre from Bac arrived at San Ignacio, deathly ill. He had been one of Padre Campos' good friends, and it was a sad day for Campos when he had to say his requiem Mass.

Padre Kino, always petitioning the provincial for more priests for his Pimas, would have been sadly discouraged by the losses if he had not been too busy to think about them. He was building two new churches, one at Remedios, another to replace the burned one at Cocóspora. They were magnificent structures, too, not the small adobe ones with which you would expect him to be satisfied. As laborers he had the best the Pima country afforded. Chief Coro came with his workers. Everybody who could handle a tool of any kind came from Bac. Chiefs rallied with their subjects from every direction, coming with their whole families to stay as long as the padre needed them.

To take care of these multitudes he collected enough corn, wheat, cattle, and clothing to feed and keep them warm. The forests furnished timber for framework, sills and flooring. Thousands of adobe bricks were made "and high and strong walls erected for two large and good churches, with their two spacious chapels, which form transepts, with good and pleasing arches." So Padre Kino described them.

During the year required to build the churches he rode each week over a hundred-mile circuit and when they were ready for dedication he added up the cost: "Five hundred beeves for consumption during the construction of the buildings, five hundred bushels of wheat and about three thousand dollars worth of clothing." He had obtained money for the latter by selling surplus ranch products at towns and mines all over the province of Sonora. Perhaps it was no wonder the Spanish shopkeepers and mine owners and ranchers looked covetously at his resources.

A wealthy Spaniard watched Kino's pack train plod into the plaza at Bacanuche one afternoon, marked the skill with which the mules were packed, saw the silver paid him for the loads of wheat and corn he had brought from Dolores. Kino himself looked like a refugee from an Apache attack, his black robe worn and dusty, his flat, wide-brimmed black hat out of shape and stained by sudden rains.

"This Kino is a fool!" said the Spaniard to a companion. "Thousands of dollars worth of goods pour out of the mission properties. Kino spends every centavo on the Indians—great churches, prosperous ranches, houses better than my creole servants have to live in—"

"Certainly he has a corner on all the free labor in Sonora," said the other wryly. "You and I could build beautiful houses for ourselves if there were only some way to get around this order protecting the Indians."

"It is not right." The wealthy man's face darkened with anger. "Indians were born to be slaves. We Spaniards are a superior race. We are supposed to conquer and subdue the natives."

"Have you ever tried to tell Padre Kino that?" said another voice and the two whirled to see Captain Manje smiling at them, a smile that broadened as he saw their expressions. "My friend, the padre," he went on blandly, "contends that an Indian is a man with a soul, that he is not to be enslaved, but converted by the preaching of the Gospel, and that those of us who are more powerful should be his friends!"

"And you agree with him, I suppose!" said the wealthy Spaniard hotly. "How did you feel about slaves last week, when you could not find enough workers in all Bacanuche to make adobes for your new store?"

Manje's dark eyes narrowed. "And when I did find laborers, I had to pay them twice as much as I expected. No doubt you know that, too? Well, it is like this: when I go to Mass on Sunday, I can see that Padre Kino's argument is reasonable, that I should treat the Pimas with Christian charity. On Monday I grow impatient with the slowness of the work and

I think a little slavery—just a little, mind you—might be a good idea!"

"You might as well stay in the church all the time." The wealthy Spaniard laughed shortly. "As long as the Pimas live near the missions the padres will pamper them and defy any of us to do anything about it."

Chapter 11

PLAN FOR NEW SPAIN

[1705]

Padre Kino rode slowly down the sandy trail from Remedios to Dolores. He did not know why he should be so tired. He was returning from a routine trip of inspection and everything was doing well this spring of 1705, the wheat green and thick in the fields, white clouds of blossoms in the orchards, and the desert gullies alight with pale yellow blooms.

Since the autumn before, worries had crowded in upon him. The gossips were causing more trouble than ever. Last September a story ran through Sonora like fire crackling through the dead branches of a tree— Chief Duck Tail of Cocóspora was plotting rebellion.

"With the staff of office I am not a man. With weapons I am one!" That was what the good-natured chief was supposed to have said. And, ridiculous as it was, Kino had to take him and his two sons (good cowboys both, and needed with the cattle) to Cucurpe for a hearing. The moment the Spaniards saw Duck Tail they knew how foolish the story was. But to make sure everyone might know the loyalty of the Pimas at Cocóspora, Kino held the Christmas celebration there in the beautiful new church, and invited every soldier within riding distance to come and share in the festivities.

Now there was more trouble afoot. Padre Kino struck the pommel with a gloved fist. He would like to get his hands on the newly appointed lieutenant who had gone to Tubutama, had threatened the Indians and had driven some of them away from the mission. The padre there was on his way to protest to the Father Visitor about it. Many of those Indians had moved their families from long distances to be closer to the church, the mission supplies. It was an arrangement of mutual advantage to people and Church.

Kino looked ahead into the cool shade of the canyon. His horse threw up its head and whinnied and there was the thunder of hoof beats as a band of mares and colts swept toward them. Kino waved his arms and shouted and his foreman rode from behind to turn the band and head the animals back to their pasture. Someone was not watching the gate—or had not mended the fence when it needed it.

The horse quickened his step. Food and water were just ahead. But before they came out of the trees there was a shrill halloo from the bluff. One of the ranch foremen came sliding down in a cloud of sandy dust, hit the trail at a run and came gasping up to throw his arms around Kino's black clad leg.

"Do not let them take me," he cried. "I do not want to leave the mission!"

"What are you talking about? Who is going to take you away?" but even as Kino spoke, he knew what had happened. The brash lieutenant had taken advantage of his absence to raid Dolores.

Kino laid the whip on the horse's side and plunged up

the trail out of the canyon, the Indian running alongside, clinging to his stirrup. The plaza was a mass of Indians, the women crying, men waving their arms and shouting their grievances to the blue sky. When they saw Kino they surged toward him in a shouting wave that sent his horse up on its hind legs, pawing the air. Kino brought him down with one blow of his gloved hand between the ears, then quieted the mob with his right hand outstretched, tracing the sign of the Cross above their heads.

Pointing to Marcos, now grown and a minor official of the village, Kino said, "What happened?"

Marcos gulped. "The officer came yesterday morning. He asked how many in the village had moved here from other places. He said we bribed them to come to Dolores. He made all of them go away with him!"

"How many did he take?" The padre's face was pale with anger.

"Ninety," said Marcos.

"Did he not question the people before he took them away?" asked Kino.

Marcos nodded indignantly. "All except three told him they came here because they wanted to. He took them anyway."

"Tell the people to go to their work," said Kino. "I will ask for an investigation." Ask, indeed! He would demand to know by what right a Spanish officer interfered with the work of a padre!

Before the investigation caught up with him, the lieutenant was far north in Arizona, on the San Pedro River, requisitioning supplies of corn from the Indians. When they did not want to give it to him he took it anyway, boasting that he had obtained the lieutenancy of this Pima land for this very reason.

Chief Coro was there and Coro knew very well what this kind of oppression led to.

"Do you want the Pimas to run away into the mountains?" he demanded. "Do you want them to join the Apaches?"

Furious at the impudence of a mere Indian, the lieutenant hurried back to San Juan to report that Chief Coro had joined forces with Chief Duck Tail. They were marching down through Sonora. The missionaries must flee for their lives!

Soldiers from San Juan started for the scene. Fortunately, Kino heard about it and intercepted them at Bacanuche, told them it was a false alarm, and sent them on to Cocóspora to see for themselves. Chief Duck Tail welcomed officials and soldiers with his customary broad grin and gave orders for a feast in their honor. Then Kino rode in and sent for Coro who came promptly with a number of his people. Shortly after his arrival a cloud of dust heralded the approach of hard-riding troops and the Flying Column pelted in from the mountains to the east.

"What is all this about?" cried the officer in command. "My orders were urgent. We were told the Pimas were in revolt everywhere, that there was another massacre of the padres."

"It is as you see," said Padre Kino, "but, since you are here, come with us to Dolores for Holy Week. Then we will send these two Pima chiefs to San Juan to see the general."

Duck Tail and Coro returned from San Juan with many gifts of clothing, hats, knives and ribbons. They then went back to their villages well content, pleased to have been the center of so much attention.

Kino too was content. The indiscreet lieutenant had gone too far, even for the men who for selfish reasons of their own had arranged his appointment. He was relieved of his duties and Kino heard no more of him. Best of all, the Indians who had been taken away began to drift back to the missions and soon all was as it had been.

But the incident left scars. The investigation had revealed that many Spaniards in Sonora would like to see the missions destroyed, the Indians left without the padres to protect them.

Yet it seemed the missions had never been stronger. Padre Kino sat at his table one day studying a request from the new provincial in Mexico City—none other than his old friend, Salvatierra. There was also a new Father Visitor, Padre Picolo, who had worked with Salvatierra in California. Kino could not have had two more staunch supporters.

At last, workers were coming from Spain. "And I beseech you," wrote Picolo, "to please inform me how many are the missions founded in Pima country and how many fathers are necessary."

Gladly Kino picked up his pen, beginning his report with the nine missions already active.

"Dolores, Remedios, and Cocóspora are under my personal care," he wrote. "Padre Campos continues at San Ignacio, with Magdalena and Imuris under his supervision. Padre Minutuli has Tubutama, and two smaller missions on the Altar River."

All these places were known to Salvatierra. Would he remember those he saw on his trip over the divide to the north? And west, to Caborca?

When he finished, Padre Kino had requested five new padres to take over fifteen villages. He dispatched the report to the Father Visitor and from there it went swiftly to Salvatierra, thence to Rome. And Padre Picolo wrote to Kino:

"In spite of the Devil, who seeks confusion, those apostolic missions are going to be founded and advanced."

In previous letters to the capital, Kino had mentioned the ranch at Sonoita, from which he hoped to drive stock to California. And he had discussed a land route to a port on the Pacific Coast, where the ship which sailed every year from China to Mexico might find harbor, and send part of its cargo over a direct overland supply route to Sonora.

And in his Historical Memoirs, which he had been writing for years at the request of his superiors, Padre Kino was making a master plan, not only for Sonora and New Spain, but for the whole continent of North America.

"At the same time the missions spread the Faith, they promote Christian civilization," he wrote. "Here they have protected Sonora from the inroads of Apaches and their fellow bandits. A mission at Quiburi, with a fort there for defense, for example, would help Chief Coro in his valiant fight against the enemy."

Kino read the last paragraph to Padre Campos one summer afternoon, while the village drowsed around them. Campos smiled at the sound of Coro's name. If Padre Kino could be said to be partial to anyone, it was that doughty old chief Coro. He couldn't be blamed for that. Coro worshipped the ground Kino walked on and had risked his life more than once in battle against Kino's enemies.

"Their Imperial Majesties will surely see the wisdom in what you write," Campos agreed. "But what of the rest of it? You said you had plans for the country beyond."

Kino's gray-blue eyes, sun-wrinkled at the corners, gazed past the patio wall with its sheltering branches, heavy with their juicy burden of golden apricots. He was seeing the land across the Gila and, in the east, the missions of New Mexico, bought by the blood of martyred Franciscan friars.

"By new missions we can add new provinces to the realm,"

he said slowly. "With the favor of heaven we shall be able shortly to enter upon the conversion of the neighboring Apaches."

"The Apaches?"

Kino nodded. "We sent messages to those who live near the Colorado River, in the north. They have invited us to come and see them. There are reports that they will be won to our friendship and to the desire of receiving our holy Catholic Faith."

Campos drew in his breath sharply. "If that were true—"

"It would mean we might enter and trade with New Mexico and with the Moqui and the Zunis." Kino's face was radiant with the dream. "From New Mexico we could go north and northwest, west to Upper California and to the Pacific Ocean. And east we could join with our fellow Jesuits in New France. A road to Canada would offer a short cut to France and Spain, only half as long as the road which we are accustomed to travel by way of the City of Mexico."

Unconsciously his hand was tracing a map as he spoke and the scientist in him was uppermost for the moment, for he hated the foolish errors in the ancient charts.

"If we continue with the promotion and advancement of these new conversions we should be able to make accurate maps of North America, the greater part of which is unknown, or practically unknown. For some ancients blot the map with so many and such errors and with such fictitious grandeurs and feigned riches as a crowned king whom they carry in chairs of gold, with walled cities and with lakes of quicksilver and gold or amber, and of corals. But they do not say a word about the principal riches that exist there, the innumerable souls ransomed by the most precious blood of our Redeemer, Jesus Christ."

Campos blessed himself, heart warm toward the sturdy Kino who, whatever else his talents might be, was first and always a missionary. The padre was thinner than he had been, Campos thought, but the country and the work did that to all of them. And Kino never ate properly, seeming to prefer an unappetizing dish to a filling, delicious one. And he still spent more hours on his knees than he did sleeping at night. He had not done so much traveling of late, however. It would be well if he gave it up altogether and saved his strength.

But when Campos said as much, Kino shook his head. "Have you not heard? Despite all we have proved, there are those who still cling to the notion that California is separated from the mainland by a great Sea, running many hundreds of miles to the north. There is still much to be done."

Late in the autumn Padre Campos read a report by a Franciscan friar who had accompanied Kino on a final trip to the head of the Sea of California.

"In shape," wrote the friar, "the head of the Gulf of California resembles the right foot of a man. The mouth of the Colorado River corresponds to the big toe. Therefore, California is not an island, but only a peninsula, as long since very well and correctly has been said by Father Eusebio Francisco Kino."

That should settle it, thought Campos, but it probably wouldn't. There was always someone who clung to the old ideas and refused to change. Look at Kino's military friend, Manje, for instance. Of all the Spanish in the New World, he had traveled most with Padre Kino, and while he had not gone on the later trips, he must have seen enough of the country to the northwest to make him give up the theory that California was an island. Give it up he would not!

Padre Campos sighed unhappily. Manje was a general now.

He had acquired a good deal of property and spent most of his time in the company of wealthy Spanish ranchers and mine owners. Had he forgotten all the lessons Padre Kino had taught him? Had he forgotten especially what fine citizens these Pimas were, wondered Campos? He had heard a rumor (Kino refused to believe it) that General Manje wanted to take these good Christian Indians and make slaves of them.

Chapter 12

GENERAL MANJE WRITES A REPORT

[1705]

A cross the mountains, in the town of Bacanuche, General Juan Manje sat in the spacious *sala* of the mayor's house one late December afternoon in 1705 and looked about him at a handful of prosperous Spanish gentlemen. They had heard rumors of what Manje was up to and every one of them hoped the rumors were true. They listened expectantly as he began to speak.

"Senores," he said, "I asked His Honor, the Mayor, to bring you here for a special purpose. As you may have heard, I have been writing a report. The last section of it consists of a list of complaints. I believe that they concern not only me, but each of you, as well." He cleared his throat and tucked his greatcoat around him against a wayward draft.

"In my report," he went on deliberately, "I have described the Pima missions, and told of their need for more missionaries—"

"What?" cried a handsomely dressed man across the room. "If you ask my opinion, we have too many of them now!"

General Manje said piously, "You must admit that Padres Kino, Campos, and Minutuli have done a great work among the Pimas."

"But, General," sputtered the mayor, "that is not what I heard you—" he stopped at Manje's upraised hand.

"I have also written," he said, "that the Jesuits monopolize the best agricultural lands, leaving to the Spaniards only the poorest, a reason why many of us are unable to maintain ourselves."

"True, true." The murmur went around the row of richly dressed Spanish gentlemen.

"There should be a remedy!" cried one of them, tugging impatiently at his glossy black beard.

"I have a remedy." General Manje looked down at the pages in his hand. "We all know that in some of the older missions the Indian population has greatly declined, so that some of them have a superabundance of lands. In some missions where at first there were ten thousand Indians, now there will be a hundred."

A covetous gleam appeared in the dark eyes of a ranch owner. "I am sure that must be true at Dolores," he said. "The last time I was there the population seemed greatly decreased—and it would be such a pity for those fine fields to be neglected."

General Manje shook his head. He would like to keep Padre Kino out of this. For the present, at least, Dolores must be left severely alone.

"The government ought to survey the mission lands," he said, "leave generous fields for the Indians, and assign the rest to the Spaniards."

His listeners gasped at the audacity of the proposal as the general went swiftly on, "After all, we have defended the province at the cost of our estates, with horses, shield, arquebus, and other arms. Since the establishment of the

Flying Column thirteen years ago, of course the citizens have left the fighting to the soldiers, but they should be given lands for agriculture to reward them for past services. And besides, we should have the same privilege granted to the settlers of New Mexico."

The ranch owner swore in delight. That meant all the free Indian labor a man needed. What an empire he could build for himself if he could make slaves of these Pimas as the Spanish of New Mexico had enslaved the Pueblo Indians. But did Manje dare carry out this plan? What about the Jesuits? How was he going to deal with them?

Manje had worked this out too, it appeared. "The Jesuits," he said, "devote all their attention to the Indians, even though most of the Spanish of Sonora lack spiritual care. Imagine a state as big as this one, twelve hundred and fifty miles around it, and only three priests to minister to us. Sometimes a year passes between visits of the priest, leaving Spaniards without Mass, confession, or communion," he read solemnly. "More parish priests are needed. Anyone can see that."

The mayor broke in, "The Bishop of Durango will send priests of his diocese to parishes if enough money is forthcoming to build churches and pay expenses."

"Who can afford to pay such expenses?" grumbled the rancher.

"We will be able to afford it if my proposals are carried out," said General Manje. "I have one more to offer for your approval," and he read, "Finally, to encourage mining, these Indians who have been Christian for twenty years or more ought to be assigned for labor for the Spanish miners. In this province there are no slaves or other people to work the mines unless it be Indians."

The mine owner touched a lace handkerchief delicately to

his nose and murmured, "I am sure the time limit must be up on the royal order protecting the lazy creatures."

The mayor was beaming again. "A splendid work!" he cried. "Senores, we are fortunate in having such a man as General Manje among us. This report of his will have far-reaching results, I am sure."

Manje eyed him. "I have had copies made for the Royal Audencia at Guadalajara and for the Bishop of Durango. To give them the proper emphasis, I think it would be well for each of you to sign these complaints. Then the officials will know that I am informing them of a public grievance."

With some reluctance the mayor took the pen and inscribed his name. The others followed, each wishing he could get out of it somehow, but unable to think of an excuse. Manje's agent, Romo, was last to sign. Then they went out into the brisk winter sunshine, each to his own home, and for the next few weeks waited uneasily to see what would happen.

Messengers were swift, but distances great and official procedures ponderously slow. It took some months for news of Manje's report to reach the ears of the Jesuit Father Visitor. Besides the parts Manje had read to his friends, he had aired the controversy between the Jesuits and the Bishop of Durango and made it appear that the Jesuits were entirely in the wrong. Padre Picolo read the report, sat himself down and wrote to the governor of Sonora protesting the calumny.

"If something is not done about this," he finished, "I will order all the father missionaries to leave the province!"

The governor was shocked and frightened. If the Jesuit padres left Sonora there might be another bloody Indian uprising. That must be prevented at all costs. General or no general, Manje had no business stirring up trouble like this. The governor ordered him arrested and brought to Parral, a capital city of the northwest province of New Spain.

One bright spring afternoon not long after Manje's arrest, a small boy at Dolores sought Padre Kino and found him at the corrals, directing the Indians as they cut out cattle for the ranch at Cocóspora. His faded black robe was patched and dusty, his weather-lined face smeared with dirt.

"You say someone must see me? It is urgent?" Kino looked at the milling herd, gave a few crisp instructions to a foreman and headed for his house at a half trot. There were a thousand things to do at this time of year around the ranches, but an urgent message from one of his Pimas could stop him any time.

It was, however, no Indian who waited in the little whitewashed *sala*, but a well-dressed Spanish lad. Padre Kino frowned, but the boy jumped to his feet before the padre was through the door.

"Have you heard what has happened?" cried the boy. "Do you know what they have done to General Manje?"

"No," said Kino calmly, "no, my son. What has happened to my friend, Manje?"

"Your f-friend? Then you have not heard about his report?"

Kino shrugged. "I have not read it, but yes, I have heard about it. Manje is young. All you young people are apt to grow a little rash. Perhaps he wrote some unwise things, but I am sure no harm will come from them in the end. Now, if you will excuse me, the men are waiting. I must get back to them."

"Will you let General Manje rot in jail, then?"

"Jail? What jail?"

So, Padre Kino had not heard! His father, the Senor Romo, had been right to send him to Dolores, thought the young man, and swiftly recounted the details of the shameful arrest. "And they sent a mere corporal to arrest General Manje, put him on a strange mule and led him back to Parral—five hundred miles to Parral, Senor Padre, and they would not even let him ride his own horse. And now a senor captain is at Bacanuche, asking questions of everyone. My father is the general's agent and him the captain questions most of all. My father says that General Manje must have your help."

"Of course." Padre Kino nodded. There were orchard trees to prune, the grass was springing green in the pastures, and all the fences had to be repaired. There were horses to round up and calves to brand. And many Pimas would be here for Mass tomorrow. But he would write the Father Visitor, ask him to put in a good word for young Manje.

"Go home," he said kindly. "Tell your father I will do what I can."

Young Romo rode away from Dolores marveling at what he had seen and heard. This shabby padre with a dirty face the richest man in Sonora? That was what his father, the Senor Romo, had said when he sent his son on this mission. "Padre Kino is the richest, most powerful man in Sonora," those had been his very words.

Young Romo had been trained to carry out orders without asking questions, but that morning a question had burst from his lips, "My father, if General Manje quarrels with the Jesuits, is it likely that one of them will help him?"

"Go quickly, my son," had come the answer, "for it is Padre Kino's habit to embrace those who mistreat him!"

Whether it was Kino's influence or not cannot be proven. Perhaps the governor felt Manje had been punished enough for the trouble he had caused. At any rate he was ordered out of jail and told to return to his home without saying any more about the matter. The hot-blooded general would have none of that. He met the governor in the plaza shortly after his release and poured out his rage at—of all people—the Jesuits.

"They are too sure of themselves. I had a letter from Sonora saying that as soon as I was made a prisoner the Jesuits brought all the Indians together and told them they could do anything they wished—and they cited my arrest as an example."

"Can you prove that?" asked the governor.

"I certainly can!"

"Produce the letter, then."

"I do not wish to do so," said Manje defiantly.

The governor met anger with anger. "You will show me the letter or you will go back to jail!"

"You may do as you please, even to cutting off my head," flared Manje, "but in that case you may look for the revolt and loss of the whole province of Sonora."

It sounded like an idle threat to the governor. Back to jail went Manje. And this time he stayed there until by some means peace was made with the missionaries he had attacked. A long time afterward he prepared a revised edition of the offensive report, omitting the complaints against his Jesuit friends, but adding that because of the stand he took, "part of the reforms which I urgently requested were made as a necessary remedy."

If it were not Kino who interceded in Manje's behalf, then why did the general go on to speak so well of the padre? Certainly whatever breach there was between the two of them was completely healed. How could it be otherwise? Manje might have grown stubborn, calculating, even a little greedy as his worldly goods increased, but he could not help loving this padre who "made it a habit to embrace those who mistreated him."

Chapter 13

THE CHAPEL OF ST. FRANCIS XAVIER

[1711]

Blackbirds fluttered their red wings along the irrigation ditches and their gay chattering rose above the gurgle of the water. The sweet smell of a cottonwood grove in the spring sun came to Padre Kino's nostrils as his horse paced easily along the road toward Magdalena. This would be a pleasant trip, and a joyous occasion, dedicating the chapel there to the padre's patron, St. Francis Xavier.

In this year of 1711 spring work pressed as always, but the Pimas could keep it going for the few days Kino would be away. All the ranches were prospering and it was fitting that he pause to offer thanks to God for the celestial favors showered upon him throughout these years among the Pimas.

He turned in the saddle and motioned to Marcos to ride up beside him. "It was at this very time of year I came here," he said. "Twenty-four years ago I rode for the first time through this pass we are approaching. The good padre from Cucurpe was with me. We established three missions before returning to Dolores."

He was silent once more and Marcos dropped back a little way. He too had been thinking. How long had it been since the padre took him over the long, exciting miles to the City of Mexico? More than fifteen. One of Marcos' own sons was as old as he had been on that momentous expedition.

Marcos thought proudly of that son. All the children were in school, but the oldest was brightest of all. He might even be governor of Dolores someday. After all, Marcos himself was a councilman.

As he so often did, Marcos wondered about his people in the old pagan days. Five years of age when Padre Kino came, Marcos remembered little of what went on then, but he had heard the old ones talk of famine, of freezing cold on winter hunts in the mountains. He fingered the sleeve of his woolen coat and thought with pity of the Indians who had lived little better than wild animals.

It was a proud thing to be a Pima. Look at Dolores and its ninety families, with every man trained in a special skill. Marcos's brother was a blacksmith, one of his cousins a carpenter; another operated the water mill. The village had its own officials, ran its own affairs. They had built a beautiful church with bells and choir chapel, with ornaments and chalice of pure gold. There was a good house for Padre Kino, too, with plenty of room to entertain visitors. And the orchard was the talk of all Sonora with its pomegranates, peaches, pears and figs, its grapes hanging in purple bounty on vines trimmed each winter by another of Marcos's brothers.

Marcos looked ahead at Padre Kino, heart swelling with love for this man who had come not only to bring the Faith, but also to teach the Pimas how to live like civilized men.

"May he never leave us," said the Pima softly. "May the good padre live forever!"

A sudden exclamation from behind made Marcos look up. In the blue sky above the rim of mountainside a buzzard tilted on widespread ragged wings, turned, soared and was joined by two more. As the little party climbed through the pass, Marcos's quick eyes saw a half-devoured carcass at the edge of the mesquite trees. A mountain lion had killed a deer and the scavengers of the sky were cleaning up what was left.

An old man in the rear said with a note of foreboding, "When I see them, I think of Caborca."

Marcos grunted. Over and over he had heard the story of Padre Saeta, the massacre, the war. He seldom thought of it any more; there had been peace for so long among the Pimas. But the old ones remembered. This one did not like the buzzards.

Kino saw the black birds too, and remembered. But, like Marcos, he had too much to think about to dwell on that long-ago sorrow. He could not recall a time when the Jesuits were not under attack from someone. At the moment it was the Bishop of Durango who demanded their expulsion. What was worse, it was reported that the King had yielded to his demand. Padre Kino did not believe it. But now he sent a swift prayer heavenward.

"Most glorious apostle to the Indies, St. Francis Xavier," he said, "protect us, protect thy people, these good Pimas!"

Magdalena was in festive garb for the occasion and Padre Campos wasted no time in taking Kino into the new chapel to show him the statue of the great St. Francis. Padre Velarde, who now assisted Padre Kino, was there too. That night the three Jesuits burned their candle down to the dish, recalling

Kino faded in the arms of Father Agustín de Campos.

the past with its tragedies and joys, speaking with gravity of the uncertain present, about which Kino, at least, refused to be pessimistic.

Santa Maria, on the divide between Sonora and Arizona, was now equipped, he reported, and Velarde boasted proudly, "New vestments with which to say Mass, three hundred head of cattle for their ranch, one hundred head of sheep and goats, a drove of mares, a drove of horses, a house in which to live, the church half finished—why, the house is even furnished."

"What about Quiburi?" asked Padre Campos.

"One person offered five thousand dollars in goods and silver for the founding of the church, house, and fortification of the great mission of Quiburi where Captain Coro lives." Kino had a pleased smile on his face. His friend Coro was appreciated, at last.

Velarde looked at him appraisingly. Kino himself had offered to finance new missionaries, if only they could be sent. And he continued to pour a flood of supplies into the California missions. There seemed no end to the bounty from this fruitful land of the Pimas, Velarde thought, as there seemed no end to the achievements of Padre Kino. He was a great man, this humble padre. He had explored and opened to Christian settlement the vast lands from Dolores north to the Gila River, northwest to the Colorado, west to the Sea of California, and in the doing had discovered a land passage to Lower California. His Indian missions were models to be copied throughout the New World and his brilliant maps were prized both here and in Europe.

But his labors had taken their toll. There were shadows under the blue-gray eyes tonight and he had grown so thin he was almost transparent.

"Let us go to bed," said Velarde, "and for one night, Padre Kino, will you sleep in a good bed, instead of those calfskins on the floor?"

Kino shook his head. He was used to the floor, with a pack saddle for a pillow and a blanket such as the Indians used pulled over him for warmth.

The next morning, garbed in beautiful vestments, Padre Kino stood before the altar. The little chapel was jammed with Pimas, come from miles distant for the dedication. The statue of St. Francis Xavier had been carried in solemn procession around the plaza. Now it was installed in its place beside the altar.

Bells chimed and Padre Kino's thin brown hands raised the Host slowly, reverently, triumphantly above his head. The crowd hushed, scarcely breathing. The richly ornamented golden chalice was lifted, set again upon the altar. Then, in the very Presence of His Lord, Padre Eusebio Francisco Kino sighed and crumpled to the floor.

A little after midnight he was dead.

The gay decorations of Magdalena were swathed in somber black and the people mourned. He was buried there at Magdalena, in the chapel of St. Francis Xavier, on the Gospel side. "For it seemed," said Padre Velarde, "that the Holy Apostle to whom he was ever devoted, was calling him, in order that, being buried in his chapel, he might accompany him, as we believe, in glory."

That same day across the divide, at Quiburi, Chief Coro woke with a start. What had disturbed him? There was no sound, but someone had spoken in his ear to wake him.

He got up and went to the door of his house. The sky was beginning to lighten. A shadowy figure moved at the edge of the village, and another. Apaches!

Coro gave the war cry, snatched his quiver of arrows, his bow, and dashed boldly toward the nearest enemy. They grappled hand to hand, swaying back and forth across the cleared space just beyond the houses. All around them the fighting raged. Coro struggled vainly to loose the iron grip about his throat, reached for the throat of his assailant—

The men of Quiburi were gaining, forcing the Apaches back. There were cries of victory as the enemy broke and ran, to fall one by one under the arrows of Coro's men. But even as they returned from the bloody chase, chanting their count of Apaches dead, brandishing bloody scalps, they came upon the body of Chief Coro at the edge of the village, and the Apache whose bitter grasp had not relaxed even in death.

Chief Coro too had fought his last battle. And, as Velarde mused on Kino's passing, so Padre Campos when he heard of Coro's death, wondered if Padre Kino had not paused long enough, on his way to heaven, to take his old friend with him.

Kino's tomb with its statue of St. Francis Xavier became a place of pilgrimage. From Arizona, from Sonora and places far beyond, people came to pray. And although the chapel crumbled and the Jesuits were banished, the good Franciscans took their place and built a new church at Magdalena.

Dolores, Mother of Missions, is gone, the place where she stood on a hill above the river marked only by a few crosses, a thicket of mesquite. The other churches Padre Kino built have long since been replaced. At the place that he called San Xavier del Bac, south of Tucson, Arizona, on the foundations Kino laid in 1700, a Franciscan church rises white, incredibly beautiful, out of the desert. Built by Indians, decorated with their finest art, it is Indians who are summoned by the bells of San Xavier to Mass. And in Sonora, to the south, the church bells also ring for them. So Kino's greatest gift to his children lives on.

And there can be no doubt in the minds and hearts of Pimas who are told of him, that together with St. Francis Xavier, the first great Jesuit missioner he was named for, Padre Kino still prays for them.

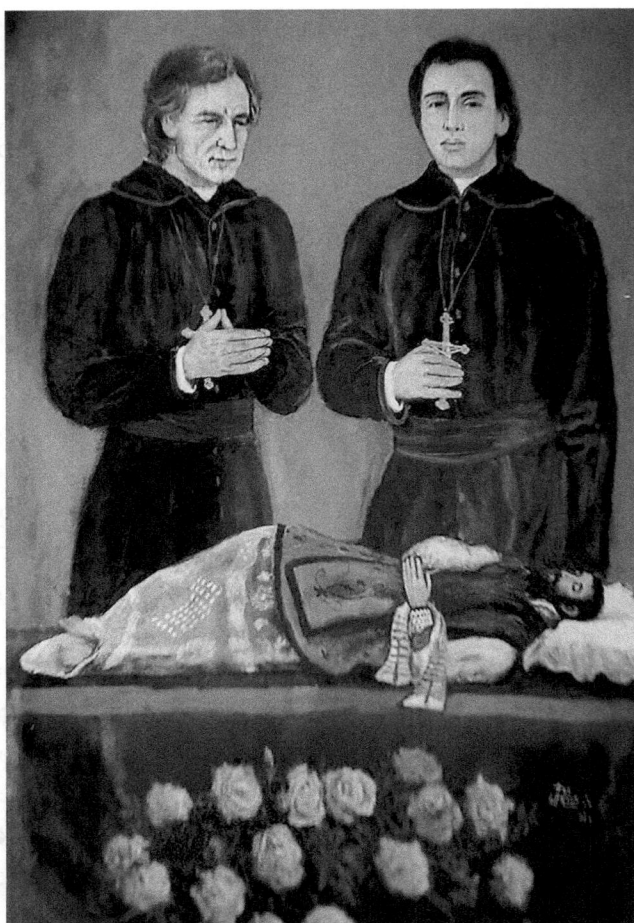

ABOUT THE ARTIST

José Cirilo Rios Ramos born in Carbó Sonora, Mexico in 1943. His nomadic family, by nature of his father's work, did not allow him to complete primary education regularly. So as an adult he completed his elementary and high school education and then continued to receive a Bachelor's in Spanish and a Masters in Teaching. He worked as a teacher for 31 years, never neglecting his self-taught passion for drawing, painting, and poetry. He also worked on many community oriented works with a local radio show and as the chair of an association dedicated to preserving and disseminating the history and culture of Sonora. He founded a regional museum and published a monthly gazette. In 1999 a mural with the history of Carbo by Ramos was unveiled in the town hall. (See a detail of it on the following page.) He created a comic called *Andanzas de Kino* and his artwork was included in a book by Giovanni Martínez Castillo called *Kino in Art*.

The art pieces included in this current edition were on exhibition at the 300th anniversary of Padre Kino's arrival in Sonora at the site of the ruins of the church built at Cocóspera. We are honored that Señor Ramos has given us permission to use his artwork in this edition.

Padre Kino—Native Advocate

Padre Kino went to Mexico City from his mission in Dolores to plead the case of the missions and the native peoples. It was 1500 miles, all done on horseback, in 53 days (see chapter 7). Here is the distance.

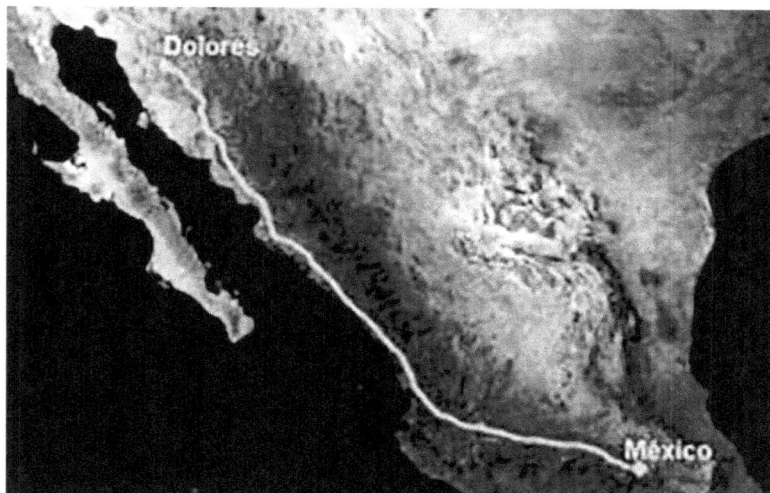

During the months that Kino worked temporarily in Mexico City, he would ride daily to Tepayac Hill in dedication to Our Lady of Guadalupe of his life and work as a missionary.

Kino's own map that he showed to his superiors in Mexico City (Fr Saeta's murder still fresh in his mind):

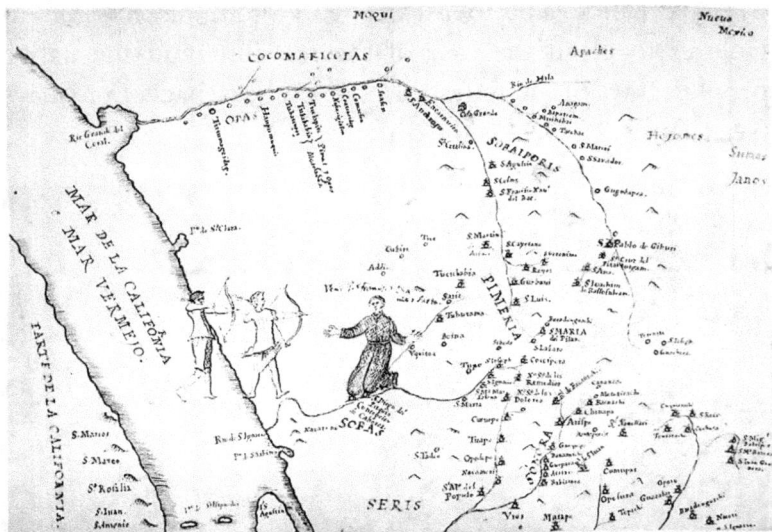

Kino Border Initiative—Kino's Greatest Legacy.

"Six organizations in the U.S. and Mexico began The Kino Border Initiative (KBI) ten years ago on January 18, 2009. Lead by Kino's Jesuit brothers, KBI provides aid to migrants deported from the U.S. and advocates for just immigration laws and humane treatment of the world's 258 million migrant people. KBI includes a national network of friends and activists. William Bole writes 'Humanizing the border has never been easy. It was hardly so in the late 1600s when the organization's namesake, Eusebio Francisco Kino — an Italian Jesuit explorer and astronomer — came to that region as a missionary and wound up defending the rights of persecuted indigenous people.'" [1]

---

[1] (Source: https://www.facebook.com/eusebio.kino.56?fref=search&__tn__=%2Cd%2CP-R&eid=ARDaodAxodmSCy5mzDz3Xgg6Ywaqj6RKEcg SJsugxhaGYajDd4vTQMb9vxUs1cPy5phutIJ_UROj7eob; accessed 2-11-19)

Author's Note

I should like to express here my deep gratitude to the people who helped so much in the preparation of this book.

Mr. and Mrs. Charles J. Farrington, of Tucson, Arizona, gave me my first glimpse of the beautiful mission church of San Xavier, founded by Padre Kino in 1700.

Mother M. Sessions, librarian at Stone Ridge, Country Day School of the Sacred Heart in Bethesda, Maryland, introduced me to Herbert Bolton's definitive works on Padre Kino and graciously allowed me to consult them whenever I wished.

Mother Sessions also directed me to the Academy of American Franciscan History, of Washington, D. C., where Reverend Finbar Kenneally, O.F.M., Ed.D., from the first gave his enthusiastic encouragement and was always willing to share his wide knowledge of the missionary period and the geographical area in which Kino worked. Reverend Matthias Kiemen, O.F.M., Ph.D., also of the Academy, gave generously of his time in clearing up some knotty problems concerning the relationship between the missionary fathers and the laity of Kino's day.

The staff at the library of the Pan American Union, Washington, D. C., gave courteous and invaluable aid in the selection of the many books made available to me from their fine historical collection.

Miss Barbara Nolen, of the staff of George Washington University, Washington, did much initial careful editing, and this was ably concluded by Miss Julie Kernan, of P. J. Kenedy and Sons, who had furnished the initial inspiration for the book.

And finally, Miss Pauline M. Papieck gave much needed and skillful help in the typing of the manuscript.

To each and every one of them, my most grateful thanks.

THE AUTHOR

Washington, D. C.
March 4, 1960

www.ingramcontent.com/pod-product-compliance
Lightning Source LLC
LaVergne TN
LVHW051349080426
835509LV00020BA/3353